Praise f
Surviving the S

"Karmela's story is moving and inspirational, and one every young person should be reminded of."

—MITCH ALBOM, Author of *The Little Liar*

"What makes a story interesting is the person telling the story... and while many people are talking about true crime these days... no one is doing it quite like Karmela and Joel Waldman. That's because of the story behind these storytellers...and that, my friends, is a story worth reading!"

— VINNIE POLITAN, Court TV Lead Anchor

"Their story is more than just a tale of survival; it's a beacon of hope and a reminder of the enduring strength found in the bonds of family, and in the courage to face life's challenges head-on. Karmela Waldman, like the tiger, is indeed an endangered species—rare, awe-inspiring, and an emblem of resilience in a world that often demands it."

— CAROLE BASKIN, CEO of Big Cat Rescue; Netflix's *Tiger King*

"Those who do not learn history are doomed to repeat it. In these troubling times, the insights of *Surviving the Survivor* offer all of us important wisdom and lessons for a better future."

— DR. AVI LOEB, Harvard Professor and Bestselling Author of *Extraterrestrial and Interstellar*

"Joel Waldman and Karmela Waldman have written a compelling hit based on their genuine, on-air conversations—frank, moving, and transformative. As they navigate the uncharted waters of podcasting, *Surviving the Survivor* goes beyond the microphone, inviting readers into the unfiltered world of a mother and son as they unravel the mysteries of their shared past and navigate the profound questions that shape the human experience."

> — DR. ANN WOLBERT BURGESS, Boston College Connell School of Nursing, Named a Living Legend by the American Academy of Nursing, and Bestselling Author of *A Killer by Design*

"Joel and Karmela Waldman's lively podcast *Surviving the Survivor* has become a must-watch for followers of true crime."

> — DENNIS MURPHY, Dateline NBC's Correspondent and Winner of Four National Emmy Awards

"As a Catholic I love that Karm survived WWII by hiding out in a Catholic school; as a comedian I love the humor in this book that by any rights shouldn't be this funny, and as someone who is currently alive, but one day will not be, I loved *Surviving the Survivor*."

> — Comedian J-L CAUVIN, Actor, Showtime's *Billions*

SURVIVING THE SURVIVOR

A Brutally Honest Conversation about Life (& Death) with My Mom: A Holocaust Survivor, Therapist & My Podcast Co-Host

SURVIVING THE SURVIVOR

A Brutally Honest Conversation about Life (& Death) with My Mom: A Holocaust Survivor, Therapist & My Podcast Co-Host

JOEL Z. WALDMAN

Post Hill
PRESS

A POST HILL PRESS BOOK
ISBN: 979-8-88845-238-7
ISBN (eBook): 979-8-88845-239-4

Surviving the Survivor:
A Brutally Honest Conversation about Life (& Death) with My Mom:
A Holocaust Survivor, Therapist & My Podcast Co-Host
© 2024 by Joel Z. Waldman
All Rights Reserved

Cover design by Cody Corcoran
Cover photo and author photo by Holly Haffner

This is a work of nonfiction. All people, locations, events, and situations are portrayed to the best of the author's memory.

Post Hill Press
New York • Nashville
posthillpress.com

Published in the United States of America
1 2 3 4 5 6 7 8 9 10

To my beautiful, sweet, smart loving family...

Ileana, Vida, Zizi, and Judah

Didn't know I could love you this much

For the two best parents any child, or adult, could ever dream of...

Roy and Karmela Waldman

Our love will never die

"All literature is an assault on boundaries."

—Franz Kafka

"For me, being a Jew means feeling the tragedy
of yesterday as an inner oppression."

—Jean Améry

"The dogs bark and the caravan passes."

—Karmela Waldman

Yea, though I walk through the valley of the shadow of death, I will fear no evil; For You are with me.

—Psalm 23 (NKJV)

TABLE OF CONTENTS

Actual Voicemail from My Mom: April 3, 2023

Jo-el, this is your mother.

Just write the fucking book. You need to just write words and not worry about it being a masterpiece. Are you really vain enough to think you're going to write a bestseller your first time? You're not Dostoevsky. Just write and stop thinking so much. It's just to have a companion to our podcast.

Alan's cancer is back.

Okay, call your sweet mother when you get a chance.

And don't forget your taxes are due in two weeks.

MIAMI JEWISH

Death lingered everywhere inside of here.

If Florida is God's waiting room, then Miami Jewish is its intensive care unit.

The hallways of this iconic nursing home, if such a description can even be attached to a place like this, extended out in every direction almost as far as the eye can see. The sterile floors glistened.

"Is this the most depressing place on planet earth?" I asked my mom.

We waited for my dad and her husband of seven decades to be wheeled back into Douglas Gardens Hospital. He was running a fever again.

Don't let the name fool you. The "Gardens" was just as heartbreaking and bleak as every other wing of this place where old Jews wait to die.

"Did you ever read *The Castle* by Franz Kafka?" my mom wanted to know. "It's about alienation. Long hallways lead nowhere."

"How do the people who work here not jump out of the windows and kill themselves?" I wondered out loud.

"You wouldn't even die because there are only two floors," my mom pointed out.

We both laughed a little. It was the only way to stay sane.

"Google *The Castle*. Aren't you embarrassed you don't know what it's about? Why did I send you to study English at Brandeis?"

Miami Jewish's walls were lined with oil-painted portraits of benefactors from a time that predated my entrance into the world more than fifty years ago—donors like Ida Cohen, Judge and Mrs. Irving Cypen, Elaine and Arthur Pearlman, and Harry and Lucille Chernin.

It was good to finally put a name to the face because my dad was living in Chernin Building, Room 216. For how long? That was anyone's guess.

I stopped and stared at the painting of Harry and Lucille Chernin.

Who were these people whose portraits hung on the walls? They seemingly had it all a half century or more ago. Money. Status. Commissioned artwork of themselves. But now what? Some were dead longer than they were alive.

Is their legacy these high-priced portraits? Buildings named after them where the eye-watering smell of boiled peas and soiled diapers wafted through the empty hallways? In a nursing home where half the residents drool in varying stages of dementia?

The absurdity of life had always fascinated my mom and me.

"Did you start writing?" my mom asked. "Here, I peeled this banana for you."

"I think I've finally figured out how to peel a banana on my own, Mom."

She was so proud I signed a contract to write this book.

"I'm afraid it'll be shit," I confessed.

Every time I thought of writing something from absolutely nothing my heart pounded with anxiety.

"Then write shit," she responded unflinchingly. "Don't be pathetic."

"Any more insults?"

"This is *not* going to be a book that future generations talk about!"

I looked up at a portrait of Hy Appleman. I wondered if anyone still spoke about him.

My mom had always insulted me in a loving way, if this makes sense, to try to squeeze the best out of me.

I was close to turning fifty-four, and here I was asking my mom how to write this very book.

"You'll never write it if you're counting on it being a bestseller."

One of the reasons my mom survived so much in life is because she never liked to stand out. She felt safer camouflaged. She was okay just being okay. I recently bought her a shirt as a joke that read, "Meh, it's okay!" with a statue of Socrates—below him his name was changed to Mediocrates.

This summed us up so well. I was unrealistically striving for Socrates-level acclaim, while all she ever wanted was to be Mediocrates.

She was just happy to be here on earth. Content to be content.

The only exception was when it came to her children. She always wanted the absolute best for my older sister, Arden, and me as well as both of our children.

My mom is a teacher, a giver, and the embodiment of a life well lived—in spite of all the pain she's still living through.

"What is the sense of looking for perfection?" she continued. "Perfection will bring you nothing if you don't actually write and finish the book."

A nurse's aide slowly wheeled an old woman past us. She stopped momentarily to adjust the green oxygen tank perilously dangling off the back of the wheelchair.

"I'm worried that once you do write this book you still won't be content. You'll try to make it even better, but, in the end, you'll just neuter it, and it will be left without a penis and vagina, metaphorically speaking of course!"

"My book is gender-non-conforming, non-binary," I joked, during a period of time when it seemed like our society had completely lost its ability to do the same.

My mom has always phrased things in a way that shocks so many others but almost never fazes me. This last comment was one of those.

"What the hell is the point of life?" I blurted out.

My mom didn't answer. She stared at me trying to prevent a smile from forming.

"I'm still formulating," she broke into laughter again. "Maybe there is no point to life. Except maybe to enjoy it."

Not a bad message for this book, I thought.

Actual Voicemail from My Mom: February 19, 2023

Jo-el,

You just called me.

[Long pause]

Call me back, handsome.

[Fumbling with the phone for a minute]

What time are you picking me up for the podcast today? I'll wait for you by the service area all by myself. I hope a stranger doesn't attack me.

Just kidding, I'll be fine. Your little, old, fragile mom will be fine.

Oh, I'm sorry, I know you hate the word "fine." I'll be excellent!

[Hangs up]

SURVIVING THE SURVIVOR

"**A**re you serious?" I asked incredulously. We had just wrapped one of our podcasts. And my mom felt the guest could've been stronger.

"Well, don't book these boring guests, and I won't fall asleep during the show," Karmela barked back, a reflexive response whenever she felt threatened or attacked.

"You nodded off in the middle of her explaining how she founded her world-famous nonprofit after the death of her daughter. She's talking about her dead fucking daughter! Everyone in the world knows her organization. She single-handedly saved an untold number of lives."

"I don't give a shit. She put me to sleep," Karm doubled down.

"You looked like a bobblehead doll. Your eyes were closed, your head was aimlessly rolling around on the base of your spine. I panicked because I didn't want to jolt you back into consciousness and make it obvious you had nodded off."

"You get one of the most boring guests on earth who is droning on about her life forty years ago. Her daughter was killed in 1980."

"So, that makes it less painful?"

"No, just more boring."

"Fine, I have a great idea. You book all the guests from now on. The stuff that comes out of your mouth is incredible, astonishing really. I do all the work, literally everything, you get all the praise and all the positive comments because you're this seemingly sweet old lady. And I have to worry about keeping you awake?"

We glared at each other.

"I just want to go home and take a hot shower." I was so annoyed.

"Why? It's not good for your skin." My mom took issue with the water being too hot. "It dries you out."

"My calves hurt from the gym." I somehow felt like I owed her an explanation for my need for a shower.

"Maybe you're pregnant and don't know it," she offered her own diagnosis about my calves being sore. "If you work out too hard, you'll end up having a heart attack and dying and then it won't matter how you look in the mirror. You always overdo it!"

"You're insane."

"Jo-el," she said, breaking my name into two syllables with her thick Hungarian accent, "if you're not happy, trade me in for a new mother."

Neither my mom nor I cared that Santi, our audio engineer, was waiting for us to stop arguing. He was used to it by now. He stood by patiently in his neon pink Lady Gaga concert T-shirt, nine-inch platform shoes, and patented black pleather pants with the seams held together by a stream of safety pins.

"You two are the best," he quipped.

"Thanks, Santi. I love the shoes." Karmela's affect and tone was now 180 degrees different than just moments ago when she was speaking to me.

She's always known how to play the crowd. And, right now, she was sweet-talking the man who made sure nothing went wrong production-wise during our true crime podcast, aptly titled *Surviving the Survivor*.

Unfortunately, preventing hosts from falling asleep during the show was not part of Santi's job specification.

Santi made the mistake of posing this question: "Karm, how are you?"

"Good. Actually, I feel like shit. I'm tired, and I have a headache from the stress of my husband. Shall I go on with my list?" she asked as we all laughed.

Surviving the Survivor, by the way, is one of the few, if any, podcasts co-hosted by an elderly mother and her middle-aged son. We launched the show in the winter of 2021 at the height of the pandemic out of sheer boredom. We pivoted to true crime after stumbling across the Dan Markel murder case. It's the story of a narcissistic Fort Lauderdale Ferrari-driving son, Charlie Adelson, who went on trial—and was convicted—this past November for murdering his sister Wendi's ex-husband Dan at the urging of his overbearing Jewish mother, Donna. Suffice it to say, while Karm and I haven't killed anyone, including each other just yet, we were drawn deep into the story because it was relatable in some weird, twisted way.

The rest, as they say, is history.

Surviving the Survivor grew to more than one hundred thousand YouTube subscribers with well over one million views per month. It also has a large following on audio platforms like Apple Podcasts, Spotify, and Audible, to name just a few.

Here's probably a good time to let you know a little bit more about my co-host Karmela.

She's a Holocaust survivor and a licensed marriage thera-pist. She also loves to curse—so much so that the marketing team who helped us with our show logo suggested we put an explicit language advisory sticker over her mouth. You know, the kind you see on albums. I loved the idea, and it stuck both literally and figuratively.

Most people simply call her Karm, a habit I'm guilty of fall-ing into too. She's also an eighty-four-year-old grandmother of eight and great-grandmother of one.

Her only grandson comes courtesy of yours truly with some help from my wife, of course. It's one of my great accom-plishments in life and one of the few things that gives me any reassurance that I'm not an abject failure. I've always felt like the black sheep in a family filled with doctors. I'm still trying to figure out my way through this puzzle that is life.

After graduating from Brandeis University, I spent years meandering before falling into a career in media after a friend suggested I apply for the NBC Page Program.

Twenty-seven-plus years later, I'm now a former cable news correspondent and past member of the so-called main-stream media.

I never thought the next step would be hosting a show with my mom.

Karm and I have always had what many describe as a unique relationship, albeit highly dysfunctional.

We love hard. But we argue and fight just as hard. I blame her for infantilizing me, while she calls me out, well, for being a pussy. Her word choice, not mine. She speaks six languages, by the way, and curses proficiently in all of them.

Karm has no patience for what she describes as my reflex-ive tendency to wallow in self-pity. She cannot stand it actually.

It is something I've admittedly engaged in a time or two, which often results in some fiery exchanges between us. Strangers have accused us of partaking in schtick. But those who know us well understand this is just us.

Our relationship is beautiful and ugly and complicated all at once. It's also unequivocally real and very deep. There's no bullshit between us. We lay it all out on the line for each other. It's an unbreakable mother-son bond built on Karm's past, my upbringing, and our lives at this very moment.

It's all so simple yet so complicated, like so much of life.

There's something else important you should know about Karm. As if the Holocaust wasn't tragic enough, she also lost her only other son when he was just three years old. I still know so little about my brother Rami, short for Abraham, because my parents, especially Karm, refused to ever dwell on anything negative. Ever. Even at the risk of coming off as callous. Neither ever willingly wanted to be trapped in negativity.

In fact, I only found out what I'm about to tell you while interviewing Karm for this very book you're reading right now.

As I was just entering into this world, my mom and dad were quietly preparing for Rami's exit. He was so sick he was sent to a place called the Lynch House in Pennsylvania, a hospice exclusively for babies and toddlers. Rami was too ill for my parents to care for him properly. He died there a short time later.

My mother had already experienced copious amounts of unimaginable loss and knew full well how cruel this world could be. It's something I was only learning now watching my eighty-nine-year-old father live his final days in a place not unlike the Lynch House.

My dad fell violently ill with pneumonia on, of all days, my mother's eighty-third birthday when he was eighty-eight. It triggered an avalanche of health issues, relegating my helpless father to a hospital bed. His once intellectually sharp mind was now blunted by an unforgiving Mike Tyson–like one-two punch combination of old age and illness.

Roy and Karm fell in love at first sight when he was a medical student at the University of Geneva. A day had rarely passed in the last sixty-three years when the two didn't kiss or hold hands. To be fair, in those many decades together, Karm would scream at my dad with near-equal frequency. My dad taught me one of the most important lessons of marriage: let the yelling go in one ear and out the other.

Another line he taught me comes from Ecclesiastes 3:20: "All go to one place; all came from the dust, and all return to the dust."

It's a line I've strangely come to rely on for comfort. It's a strategy of sorts I use to negotiate my own endless anxiety. I tell myself I too will die one day soon so don't worry so much. It works for a while. And then I'm usually right back to worrying about what to worry about.

Unfortunately, right now, there's too much to choose from: my dad's impending death, keeping my marriage healthy, or ensuring my three high-energy kids at nine, seven, and four are well taken care of after voluntarily leaving the safety of a twenty-seven-year career in broadcast news.

My mom was saddled with sadness in the face of another inevitable, life-altering loss. This one, without her husband by her side, without a doubt will be the hardest to take.

"I feel like, who is going to save me? Who is going to love me?" she recently confided in me about the prospect of losing her husband.

For Karm, losing her Roy was worse in her own mind than the tragic loss of her own father in the Holocaust or the loss of a child more than fifty years ago. The love of her life was dying and a big part of her was too—on the inside.

Still, she refused to show it. I knew she was a Survivor with a capital "S." But I had never actually seen her survive in real time—until now—when she was most vulnerable.

Her world was stopping, but she kept moving. She went to the nursing home. She laughed with the nurses. She screamed at them too. They laughed with her. But no one screamed back at her. They could see how tough she is. They had a sense she had been through so much more.

Karm is the personification of strength, resolve, persistence, and—arguably most important—optimism.

It was during this time that it hit me—my mother is a gift.

Not only did her stories need to be shared but so did she.

Karm has such a unique perspective on Life with a capital L: love, happiness, humor, money, marriage, family, our obsession with social media, mental health, death, the importance or lack thereof of getting a *New York Times* obituary, and so much more.

If I could put Karm's essence into words—and how she truly looks at life—I knew I could share this rare gift with so many more than just me and my family.

The conversations you're about to hear between my mom and me are intimate, real, raw, disturbing, sometimes expletive-riddled, explosive, and emotional but always filled with love. I recorded hours and hours of our discussions, so I could present to you the most authentic Karm possible. This is really her—unapologetic, unrelenting, and often underappreciated by me.

I knew that capturing Karm's being was the most important and toughest reporting assignment I've ever had—but also, if done well, it could be the most rewarding and impactful. Not just for me but for all of you too.

But first you need to know her origin story and how much she went through before she was even five years old.

Jo-el,

At nine o'clock your father and I are watching a movie, so we will be out of commission.

Your father might try to get romantic. He still can't get enough at eighty-seven.

Okay, love you, goodbye.

KARM'S
HOLOCAUST STORY

PART ONE: THERE WAS NO BETTER FATHER ON EARTH

"I was two years old in 1941 when the Nazis marched into Yugoslavia. My father never believed the Nazis would actually invade our land and take the people we love from us."

It simply became known as "the story" in our home—what happened to my mom during the Holocaust—and it was rarely ever discussed. In fact, I cannot remember a single moment in my lifetime when my father, mother, sister, and I all talked about it together. We'd learn bits and pieces over the years whenever we or my mom would randomly broach the somewhat taboo subject. She later explained to us that she feared the label "victim" so much she preferred to stay silent. She'd rather say nothing than be perceived as being weak or vulnerable. Many Holocaust survivors were of the same mindset.

"I loved him so much. I can still remember what he smelled like."

My mom was speaking of losing her father—my grandfather—Laszlo Krishaber when he was just thirty-two years old. Seventy-nine years later, my mom's pain was still so raw you could feel how palpable her loss was as she sat in deep thought, teary-eyed while speaking into the voice recorder on my iPhone.

"He was just so sweet and smart." She paused like she was reliving a moment in a time capsule during the short period they had together. "There was no better father on earth."

This was inexplicable and unfathomable to me. I tried so hard to connect to my mother's emotional state but could never fully grasp how her wounds could still run so deep more than three-quarters of a century later.

"Sometimes such smart people can be so dumb in other ways. He didn't believe such evil could exist in our world. I'm still angry at him for not realizing this. He didn't need to die. He was taken to the gas chamber and disposed of like an old pair of shoes."

Karm was as incredulous as I in trying to understand how this could be a real story, no less about my very own mother and her father, my grandfather.

It was a conversation we'd never have had with this sort of detail and intensity if not for this book deadline. In the past, it was a difficult conversation always much easier to put off for another less stressful time. We had been great at procrastinating for the last fifty-four years since my birth.

"For all his brilliance, he was stupid." My mom wiped away a tear from her eye, admitting, despite being a therapist herself, she never dealt with her own anger about her father's untimely and cruel death. "I'm just so mad still."

Laszlo Krishaber graduated in 1931 with a degree in optometry from a prominent Germany university. The tradesman soon became a successful businessman with his own store called Optika on the corso in Subotica. Life was seemingly idyllic.

"Branding wasn't a thing back then." My mom was stalling to avoid what we both knew was coming—the story of her father being snatched by the Nazis and her forced hiding. "Optika basically just means optician in Serbo-Croatian. This was common. Our synagogue, for example, was just called 'The Synagogue.'"

Today, it has a slightly fancier name and is known as the Jakab and Komor Square Synagogue and remains, after all these years, the second largest synagogue in Europe. In 1990, the Hungarian Art Nouveau house of worship was designated a "Monument of Culture of Exceptional Importance," which means it's protected by the Republic of Serbia.

"It's a very interesting story. Two Jewish architects created the synagogue and built it. It looks like a giant gingerbread house. Jakab and Komor also designed a blocks-long city hall, which also looks like something out of a European fairy tale. Tourists travel to vacation in this part of Serbia just to see the architecture."

My mom recounted the story from the twenty-seventh floor of her Miami Beach condo. In the distance, cruise ships headed out to sea, and much closer to shore, ant-sized people littered the famous pristine white beaches below. A stark contrast to what she was about to describe during that dark, gray Eastern European winter more than seventy-five years ago.

"As my mother explained it to me later in life, our immediate family was in total, absolute denial. We had relatives two hours away by train in Budapest, which was considered a big city, at that time, with over a million people."

My mom wasn't just speaking. She was reliving a part of history she so desperately wished was never eternally attached to her in the first place. My mom was looking through those same cruise ships like they were made of glass—lost in her own disturbing reality—nervously tapping a coffee cup I had given her weeks earlier. It read "Straight Outta the Nursing Home" with her mug, quite literally, on the mug itself.

"When my mother said, 'Let's escape to Budapest and disappear because it's getting worse and worse,' my father said, 'You can go, Vera.' That was my mother's name. 'Vera, you can go Vera, but I'm not letting my daughter'—meaning me—'go with you because the Germans are a civilized people, and you are just panicking.'

"So, my mother and I stayed put, and we went out to eat at restaurants, and we went out to the lake, and my father went into the office regularly."

But there was nothing regular about any of it. This was simultaneously the beginning of the end and the end of the innocent beginning of my mom's young life.

"Tension is building in the air. Things are not going well. But your grandfather Laszlo, an eternal optimist, still believed the Germans were civilized and the Holocaust would not and could not happen."

Now it was me looking into the distance, wondering. Maybe my tendency toward pessimism didn't evolve from nothing? Was it some sort of Darwinian response to my grandfather's fatal optimism? The universe works in mysterious ways, I thought, refocusing on my mom and the story she was sharing.

"At one point they told us we must go into the ghetto. But the ghetto was in a part of town that was called the garden town, which means there were small houses with little gardens, very small houses with very nice gardens. And what happened was that you find your own place in the ghetto. And my mother and father found a family who was willing to move into town into our house. And we moved into their house. We locked a room full of our belongings in our house, and they didn't touch that room."

It was a horrifying reality show: a depraved, demented version of *House Swap* where Jewish families were forced into giving away their hard-earned homes to strangers.

PART TWO: THE NAZIS ARE COMING

My mom's gaze was no longer on those cruise ships approaching the hazy horizon. She was distracted by something else now. It didn't take much for her to get sidetracked. A sunny silhouette of a figure slowly appeared.

"That's not a job for a nice Jewish boy." She pointed to her balcony.

A disheveled, portly middle-aged man with a harness around his significantly sized waist stood perilously on a scaffold made of what appeared to be a few pieces of plywood nailed together. To be clear, he was on the *other* side of the balcony. There was nothing between him and the twenty-seven floors below except those shoddy looking slabs of wood. He looked like he should have a can of beer in his hand instead of whatever tool he was using to do his repairs.

"What would you do if I did that for a living?" I asked.

"I would be worried," my mom answered without missing a beat. She refocused herself on the story of her survival during World War Two.

"Life continues somewhat normally until June 17th, 1944. That day the mayor of Subotica called my father. They were friends. The mayor tells him, 'I heard that they're going to take away all the Jews from the ghetto tomorrow morning, so do something, disappear.'"

My mom was looking through the balcony man now, as if his presence was suddenly normal, back to retrieving information from her memory bank.

"So, my father comes home and tells my mother and grandmother about his conversation with the mayor. There are a lot of little details I can't remember."

"Yeah, I get it. It was seventy-nine years ago." I urged her on.

"My grandmother was an unbelievable person, by the way. Her name was Nagyi. She says we have to get organized. We must do something. We cannot be taken away."

Nagyi, my great-grandmother, and Vera, my grandmother, weren't as optimistic as my grandfather Laszlo about the deteriorating situation sweeping across Europe.

Vera, for whom my first daughter Vida is named, had prepared fake documents in advance for everyone. Just in case. And now *just in case* became a harsh reality.

"The Nazis were coming to take us by train from the freight station the next morning. They're going to take us away. At that point, my grandmother and mother mobilized and organized."

Though we were mid-conversation, I was having an entire other dialogue in my head.

Is this why I suffer from OCD? I wondered silently.

Ever since I can remember, my mom has been pushing me, forcing me to act, rather than bathe in emotion, always driving me to move forward, even when I have nothing else to give.

No better example of this surfaced than during the editing of this very book when I made the mistake of telling my mom how it was going.

"I'm reading this, and I can't believe it. It's pretty good and even sort of deep, I think," I relayed my most personal thoughts to her. "I'm on page sixteen."

"Don't make any changes!" My mom shrieked, "An editor already went through it. And move your ass goddamnit, move your ass. Page sixteen? There are hundreds of pages to go. Move your ass!"

I had to call my mom back to double-check some of the spelling of the Serbian names. The edit process is tedious.

"What page are you on now?" she answered the phone with extreme urgency.

"I'm on page twenty-one..."

"Jesus Christ, man! What's wrong with you? Why are you editing so slowly, man? Do you understand how slowly you're moving? What's wrong with you."

I warned her anything she might say could and would be used in the writing of this book, including during the editing process. I was trying to brush her back like a pitcher keeping the batter off home plate.

But she couldn't control her emotion. It was all done out of love. She didn't want me perseverating over words—she wanted the book written and done. She was always doing, always moving the proverbial goal posts forward, and could not handle anyone else, especially her son, not doing the exact same thing.

It all took a toll on me mentally. Is my OCD some sort of generational trauma? Am I Hitler's collateral damage? I had never pondered these thoughts until writing this now.

"My grandmother and mother—they had little pieces of jewelry. They hid it on their body. They had a little money. They hid that on their body too, along with their forged documents."

My own dad would always say "life turns on a dime." *Why a dime and not a nickel or a penny?* I wondered. Regardless, my mom's story was beginning to make me realize why. Things for her in 1944 were happening swiftly, suddenly, and scarily.

"The next morning, very early at around five thirty a.m. Hungarian—I repeat Hungarian—SS officers come to our front door. And they say, prepare all your jewelry and prepare everything else and hand it over to us and prepare a suitcase because you are going away. And, my father turns to my mother and says, 'Do something!'"

I could see a tear welling up in my mom's eye. But she didn't want me to see it drop to the table. She excelled at survival by being able to shut out difficult thoughts like the one she was recalling right now.

"That rope would be good for hanging," my mom said. She was looking at what was tethered to the balcony repair man. She always turned to dark humor to turn off the pain.

My mom collected herself. That tear welling up in her wrinkled eye disappeared.

"Do something meant save me. My father wanted his little daughter spared. And now there were only seconds to spare. There was barely enough time to react."

"I wonder if he's seen me naked," my mom posited out loud. "God, I hope not. For his sake." We both laughed.

At this point, we both felt like we should have waved to the balcony man but realized that would be too awkward even for us.

"My mother takes me by my hand. Next thing I know, we are in a garden area surrounded by homes. In the back corner there is a fence with a little door. My mom grabs my little, soft, warm hand, and we ran as fast as we could through that door. We just kept going and going."

I looked at her hand now. It was wrinkled with age spots despite being beautifully manicured. A gentle reminder that age catches up with us all. She was nervously tapping her index finger on the white tablecloth.

"As fate would have it, we were virtually on the border of the ghetto and what was considered the 'normal area.' My mother suddenly slowed her pace from a frantic run to a brisk walk. We walked and walked and then walked some more until the bottoms of our feet ached. It's like five o'clock, six o'clock in the morning."

I needed to interrupt my mom. "How come your dad didn't go with you? You said Grandma had documents for all of you?"

"No one came. They were all afraid they'd be caught right away."

That tear was reforming in her eye.

"I'll never forget this detail. My mother had on a cream color coat. Everybody else was wearing gray, brown, black. This was the war. And she got so nervous. She had mistakenly put on a cream-colored coat. She stood out when she shouldn't have."

Another reminder why mom always wanted to be camouflaged. My entire life I've wanted to stand out. I've wanted attention. It's why I chose a career as a news correspondent. I fed off being seen and admired. Not my mom.

Luckily, they were able to stay incognito long enough to reach a nearby home where my grandmother knew a woman named Maria Olga.

PART THREE: YOU DON'T HAVE TO FEAR ANYTHING

My mom's gaze out the window was broken by a wave of her hand. I looked over. He was back. The balcony repair man who had descended below our view was back perilously dangling before us. He waved back to my mom. I wondered what he'd think of my mom's story of being a survivor as he was clearly one too, for different reasons.

"My mother goes to this woman's house and knocks on her window. She had no children. She had no husband. And this woman happened to love me very much. Her name was Maria, and she knew your grandmother because they were both teachers. I had met Maria many times before."

I had never heard about Maria until now. More than fifty-four years later, since I came into this strange world, so many bits and pieces of my mom's Holocaust story remained mysterious and convoluted. I still wasn't sure if it was because she never really explained it well or because I never fully wanted to understand it, or perhaps a combination of both.

My mom called me back upset about losing her cool regarding my edits of this book.

"Don't make a caricature out of me. You're the only one I lose it with."

She was FaceTiming me distracted by news of the war breaking out in Israel. I could hear a reporter's voice blaring in the background.

"I swear I'm going to have a stroke. The one who loves you most will kill you in the end. I have a cough that will not go away. I pray I don't have lung cancer. Larry Lerner got lung cancer. He smoked but stopped sixty-five years ago. Do not make me into a cartoon character."

Both of my nieces' husbands were just called up to the reserves to go fight for Israel. While I obsessed about book edits, the two of them were on the ground in northern Israel ready to go to battle.

"The homes in Subotica were built in a way that the windows almost touched the ground," my mom explained. "So my mother knocked on the window. There was no answer, so she knocked on the window again and again. But nobody opened it. My mother understood that she was too afraid to open the window."

As Nazis infiltrated Subotica, so did an unparalleled level of fear. Most people, my mom told me, remained in their homes too scared to even come to the door or window and this included the non-Jews.

"So, my mother and I continued to walk briskly with our heads down trying to remain as inconspicuous as possible. Your Grandma Anyu had another friend from the teacher's seminary whose name was also Maria. This one was Marija Tombac."

We had always called my mom's mother Grandma Anyu. I had always thought Anyu was just her name. It wasn't until I was in my twenties that I discovered Anyu meant "mother" in Hungarian. So, in English, she was essentially named Grandmother Mother. These strange subtleties were attributable to half my family speaking a language foreign to mine.

"Grandma Anyu knocked on Marija Tombac's window. She knocked again. Nothing. Then, suddenly, the window slowly slid open."

My mom described her as a small, dark-haired woman with a comforting voice.

"Ms. Tombac told us she was going with us. And where were we going? We were going to the eye doctor who was friends with my father who was an optometrist. I had heard of Dr. Ivo Sercer before but had never met him."

I wondered how my mother could remember all these details from nearly eighty years ago. She had always chalked it up to a good memory. But it was more likely that the events she experienced at such a young age were so traumatic that they were emblazoned on her young brain, never to be forgotten.

"Dr. Sercer sounds like it's a Jewish name, but of course he wasn't. He had always told my father, 'Anything, anything I can help you with, I will help you.' Now was that time. Somehow, we made it to his house without being seen. Dr. Sercer opened his creaky door, greeted us warmly, and, most importantly, let us in."

My mom didn't even realize it, but she let out a sigh of relief.

"Dr. Sercer told my mother that he is the benefactor of a local Catholic school. He knew the Mother Superior there and explained that she was a woman of God and would help us. He said he'd be right back. As quickly as he appeared, he disappeared to seek out her help."

My own dad had always marveled at life's serendipitous nature, telling us it's a game of inches. I wondered how my life would be different or if I even ever would have had one if it wasn't for some man I had never met—and never would—who was now long dead named Dr. Sercer.

"Dr. Sercer retuned a short time later to report that they were accepting me. I was going to be sent to a Catholic school for boys. But we'd have to wait until it was dark because they didn't want anyone to see us."

The wind high atop my mom's building began whipping. The balcony repairman seemed unfazed by it as his scaffold bounced on and off against the very rail he was trying to fix while suspended in midair.

"Jesus Christ!" my mother said while watching him sway back and forth. "Is he just waiting to die?"

"Speaking of waiting to die, what's the last image of your dad?"

My mom and I often crossed what most would consider a socially acceptable level of humor, especially when we were speaking amongst ourselves. It turned out it was a short question with a long, unexpected answer.

"I have a few images of my father. I admit that some of them I confuse with photographs. But I remember as if it were today, I will never forget it, it is still in my memory that there was an upright piano in our home. He lifted me and seated me in front of it. I was a little scared of the height, but he wanted me to see him. And he said to me in Hungarian, he said to me, 'As long as you see me, you don't have to fear anything.'"

That same tear welled up in her eye again. She tried to blink it away. She stood up abruptly, walked toward the balcony repairman, and slid open her glass door to speak with him.

"Can I get you some water?"

He answered no in Spanish, pointing to a red cooler filled with Gatorade and beer.

"Are you really asking him if he wants water while he's hovering on the other side of your balcony?" I asked incredulously even though I wasn't really that surprised at all. My mom really cared deeply about everybody. She has a heart of pure twenty-four-carat gold.

During the writing of this book, she reminded me how devoted she was to civil rights her entire life.

In 1963, as a filing clerk at Syracuse University's library, while my dad was doing his residency in psychiatry, my mom befriended a Black woman named Gwen Step. They used to have long conversations about race in America. My mom knew what it felt like to be discriminated against and told Gwen she never wanted her to feel the same way. Despite being looked at strangely, my mom invited Gwen and her husband over for dinner. My parents were both active with CORE, the Congress of Racial Equality, and even marched on Washington.

"Is it a crime now to ask if someone wants water?" my mom snapped back. She refocused and got back to the business of telling me about the last memory of her father before he was snatched by Nazis at their front door before her young, toddler eyes.

"So, this kind of really stayed with me. When my father said, 'As long as you see me, you don't have to fear anything.'"

Immediately I thought of my own children. Recently my own four-year-old boy, Judah Mac, exclaimed, "Daddies know everything!" I assured him he was right. It's only later in life, thankfully, when we learn that our own parents are not infallible. My grandfather made a promise to my mom he couldn't keep. She was terrified when she saw him taken away.

"From what I was told later, my father and grandfather were sitting waiting for the cattle car. My grandmother was also nearby. Suddenly a siren went off. And my grandmother grabbed the woman sitting next to her. I have her name written down somewhere."

A running joke in our family finally made some sense. My mom kept little notes for herself everywhere. In her walk-in closet in Miami Beach, she had notes telling her where the next note was located, which would reveal her bank account number or her safety deposit code. Years after the war she remained paranoid and preferred to keep morsels of information on scraps of paper that needed to be pieced together instead of divulging too much information all at once. It made no sense, but it was still the way her mind worked. We still joke that it will be impossible for me to put her will and estate papers together once she's gone. It'll be like trying to solve a ten-thousand-piece puzzle.

"So, my grandmother grabs this woman and says to her, 'Let's run away.' And the two of them start to run and run and run. They pass a peasant woman and hide in a yard nearby. She saw everything. Two Nazis appear and ask this peasant if she saw two women. She says yes! But she points in the other direction. The Nazis take off running in the wrong direction, and that's how my grandmother survives. She made it on her own to Dr. Sercer's house and was reunited with my mother."

PART FOUR: A DEADLY LESSON

There aren't too many Holocaust stories that have a happy ending. And you can count my mom's story in that same category. Sure, she survived and so did my Grandmother Anyu and Great-Grandmother Najyi, but my Grandfather Laszlo wasn't as fortunate.

Just as my mom was getting to my grandfather's untimely demise at just thirty-two years old, even though he looked much older, incredibly the balcony repairman was gently knocking on the glass he was there to fix.

"Okay, I'm going to throw this guy off now," my mom sort of joked. She walked toward him, leaving me annoyed mid-interview knowing that my time was limited before I had to go pick my kids up at school. The story of my grandfather's gruesome murder at the hands of the Nazis would have to wait. The repairman decided he'd take my mom up on her water offer after all.

"I'm moving my derriere as fast as I can," my mom blurted as she passed me to get him some spring water from her fridge, which I was happy to see was adorned with magnets from our podcast *Surviving the Survivor*.

"Love the dedication," I told her. She ignored me and walked back to the dangling man. "Here you go, tweetie pie," my mom said, invoking a phrase she was famous for using with so many, including now the balcony repairman, as she gingerly leaned over the edge of the rail to hand him a plastic cup filled to the brim with water. He didn't speak a lick of English and had no clue what she was saying, but gladly took the water. My mom always had to have the last word. "Be careful on your way down!"

If it wasn't my kids distracting me or my mom's undiagnosed ADHD preventing a smooth interview or my wife calling with the catastrophe du jour, now I knew I could also rely on "balcony man."

It was just yesterday the school nurse called us four times in a matter of ninety minutes with reports of a banged-up nose from a basketball gone awry, as well as complaints of stomach cramps, among other ailments. The nurse told us our three children broke the school record for most nurse visits in under two hours. I was a proud father.

I had to refocus my mom once again. "So, what happened to Grandpa Laszlo?" I asked. There was no hesitation from my mom. She jumped right back into 1944.

"Grandpa, my mother's father, whom she adored, was gassed with my father."

Her distant stare was back. And, amazingly, "balcony man" had descended out of sight. We were in the clear for her to finish her story.

"Witnesses at Auschwitz later told my family that my father went over to a guard and sparked up a conversation. He believed his ability to speak German with a perfect accent would help save him. He had studied there for four years and thought that would impress the Nazi guards. He apparently even said to them, 'I could be of use if you need anybody to chisel eyeglasses.'"

It was a deadly lesson in being careful what you ask for.

"The guard immediately put him in the line for the gas chamber unbeknownst to them at the time. My grandfather joined him because they wanted to stay together. So, they were gassed together. Romantic, wasn't it? Gassed together."

My mom had always tried to lighten the mood during difficult times. She then also squeezed in a quick life lesson.

"The Nazis didn't think, 'Oh, how optimistic this guy is.' They thought, 'What does this guy think? He's a big shot?' They wanted laborers. Not well-educated optometrists."

My mom happened to be wearing her Mediocrates shirt I had just gifted her. And this is precisely why it literally and figuratively fit her so well. Unlike her father and now her son, she wanted to go unnoticed, despite her larger-than-life personality.

"My aunt and my uncle and nephews and nieces and cousins were all murdered too."

PART FIVE: A MOTHER WHO LOVES HER CHILD DOESN'T LEAVE HER WITH STRANGERS

"Well, this is cheerful so far. Nice way to spend a beautiful day in Miami Beach reminiscing about mass murder and carnage," I weighed in, co-opting some of my mom's black humor.

"This shouldn't be in your book anyway," my mom snapped back.

"Wait, what? Your Holocaust story?" I asked.

"It should just be my advice about life. This other stuff is too much," she pleaded with me, to no avail.

"Yeah, the Holocaust isn't really *that* important a part of who you are!"

My mom was finding a new way to distract herself by flipping through the pages of *Ocean Drive* magazine. We sat in a stalemate for a few moments. I knew she needed some time to collect herself before moving on with her story.

"So, what's your biggest piece of life advice?" I asked in an attempt to jump-start our conversation.

"Buy low and sell high," she offered up without missing a beat.

"So, what happened next?"

"Night falls and Dr. Sercer—who is such a soft-spoken, tall, very gentle, nice guy, a wonderful man—takes my mother and me over to the nuns."

It was impossible for me to process how my very own mother, the woman who gave birth to me, born a single generation before me, could have endured what she was describing to me. I've tried so many times to make it make sense but to no avail. It just always seems to come up short as her reality—and mine—despite it all being so horrifyingly true.

"The Catholic boys' school had an enormous gate surrounding it. The doors slowly opened, and one of the nuns came out. We didn't go in. She came out to greet us. I'm just four and a half years old. It was June 18th, 1944, and I was turning five that coming August 7th."

So many thoughts were going through my head at once.

My cell phone vibrated, and I looked down at my iPhone wallpaper, which happened to have a picture of my three children. Judah Mac, the youngest and only boy, was the same age as my mother when she was taken to the nuns. He is my baby. Even though I had known for years how old my mom was when she was taken into hiding, it hit me with such indelible force right then and there: she was a baby too.

Inches from us sat a photo of two of my mom's best friends, Bruria and Rita. Bruria had survived the Holocaust herself and became one of Israel's most prominent attorneys before succumbing to cancer years ago. Rita, a chain smoker, is alive and kicking, and also in Israel as one of the Holy Land's most esteemed architects.

Originally from Poland, Rita spent a large part of World War Two hiding in an attic away from her parents, while Bruria's story was almost too impossible to believe. She spent many nights outside tucked away inside a coffin in a backyard cemetery. As adults they'd often joke with each other about who had it the worst.

Most of her life, my mom, in comparison to her two close friends, only considered herself "sort of a survivor."

"Recently, another friend of mine, who is also the child of survivors, told me, 'Karmela, deal with it. You are not a first-class survivor. You are only a second-class survivor.'"

"What did you tell her?" I asked, hearing this for the first time. I expected that my mom was about to tell me she'd ripped this person a new asshole. My mother always fought fire with fire. But she offered up a response I didn't anticipate.

"I said, 'Fine.' I accepted what she said, but I wondered why. She told me, 'Just think of the Polish people. They were mired in the war for three or four years. Someone I knew hid inside the hollowed-out carcass of a pig that entire time.'"

Imagine being told your story of survival wasn't as difficult or untenable as another's.

"Did you have your usual urge to tell this person to fuck right off?" I wondered out loud.

"No, no, no. I felt she was one hundred percent right. I was never in a concentration camp. Her parents were in a camp for years. And I felt that my personal experience is what I'd describe as 'Holocaust-light.'"

This twisted post-genocide competition devolved into a beer-labeling contest. What a world.

"So, what happened when your mother and Dr. Sercer brought you to the Catholic school?"

"To make a short story long [one of my mom's go-to expressions], when the nun opened the door, Dr. Sercer and my mother helped me go inside. I was clinging to my mother. I wasn't five years old yet.

"And I screamed at the top of my lungs when the door closed."

I was trying so hard right then to imagine leaving Judah Mac alone with a stranger in an even stranger place. None of it translated. My attempt to truly absorb what she had been through was futile.

"'A mother who loves her child doesn't leave her with strangers,' I screamed as my young but powerful voice echoed off the cold, cement walls."

"Before your mother died, did you ever discuss that moment again?" I needed to know.

"I said it in Hungarian. I did not speak Serbian then. She remembered it forever. She remembered it. You know, she even wrote it down when she was eighty-four. She lived with guilt her whole life because of that one decision. But I'm forever indebted to her because she saved my young life."

Now I was the one with a tear welling up in my eye.

"This was a Catholic school for boys. For boys. Not for girls. They took care of orphan boys who needed care. For some reason, I remember they had very cheap soap. And it was cold there. It was not a warm environment; the walls were cold with crucifixes hanging everywhere. I think maybe they were saving on the heat. I don't know. Even though it was during the summer, it was cold. It became unbearably cold in fall."

"Did they cut your hair to look like a boy?" No matter how many times I'd heard my mom's story, it always remained fuzzy. I'd discovered that I had developed a form of selective memory. I had always believed she was forced to shave her head to fit in with the other boys, but she assured me this was not the case.

"The nuns adored me. They loved me, and they took very nice care of me. One of the nuns was assigned to me. She only took care of me. And I liked them, and they liked me."

My mom, who came from a religious Jewish family, was living in a Catholic school for boys. I wish it could compute. I desperately wanted to understand how my own mother went through this.

"They brought in the priest, and they converted me. The father even baptized me and dipped my head in the holy water. I remember how cold that water was too. Every week the priest would come in and do some religious ritual."

I was thinking something I shouldn't have been, but I couldn't help my Jewish neurotic self. "Did he ever try to touch you?"

"No, the priest never touched me. No. You are crazy. Sorry to all my Christian friends. The Mother Superior, who my mother remained in touch with her entire life, was an unbelievable woman."

One indisputable childhood memory was the beautifully framed photograph of that very same Mother Superior hanging on our pale blue walls in our living room for all our family's friends to see. Guests would often ask, "Why is there a picture of a nun?" For whatever reason, this was always a source of pride for me. The woman who saved my mom prominently displayed. She, too, was a symbol of strength and survival.

"I remember she played the piano. She told everybody that I was a refugee, part of her extended family from Croatia. Her name was Mother Matilda Goricanec.

Sometime in my thirties, I found out that my mom sent her donations until she passed in her late nineties. Mother Goricanec knew she was loved and admired.

PART SIX: JUST TRYING TO SURVIVE IN A ROUGH WORLD

Humans are weird, needy creatures. My beloved Mabel Rose, my puggle of seventeen years, left her mom and got on a plane from Missouri to Miami at just eight weeks old. Here I was fifty-four years old staring at my own mother, wondering how I'd ever survive without her. I'd depended on her for so much for so long.

"What am I going to do when you die?" I asked her bluntly, which I had done many times before, to her annoyance.

"Don't waste my time with stupid questions. You'll enjoy your own children."

How could my mom possibly have survived without her parents for nearly half a year at just the age of four and a half?

"After leaving me with Mother Goricanec, my mother and grandmother took a train from Subotica, Yugoslavia, to Budapest, Hungary. They were very afraid of being recognized, horrified really."

My own children struggle when I leave for work for a few hours. Somehow my mom said goodbye to hers without ever knowing when or if she would return.

"Eventually, my mother and grandmother were reunited with my grandmother's sister and her two daughters. They hid together using those false documents. They didn't wear yellow stars."

As painful as the separation was for my mom, it was apparently even more difficult for my Grandma Anyu.

"After a while, my mother began to really, really suffer because she missed me so much. She knew someone else who had a relative in Budapest who worked for the railroad. In exchange for a gold cross, they asked him to go and fetch me and bring me back to Budapest. At this point, I had been in the Catholic school for about five and a half months, which is a long time for a small child to effectively be left alone."

During that time, my mom told me she transformed from a precocious little girl who looked a lot like Shirley Temple with curly gold locks into a withdrawn, pale shell of herself.

"I remember, at one point, I had a stye on my eye. Luckily, it was Dr. Sercer who came to the school to treat it because I was familiar with him. But I became very withdrawn. I went from a loud-mouthed little child to an adult stuck in a tiny body forced to protect myself."

As fast as news travels now with the advent of social media, my mom grew up in a part of Europe where horse and buggy was still the main way to get around. So, getting information was equally challenging.

"My mother would periodically get updates about how I was doing, and that's why she bribed that railroad worker. He eventually arrived at the Catholic school and brought me back to Budapest."

It was a much-needed reunion. But the elation and joy turned into tears of fear as Budapest came under siege. My mother, Grandma Anyu, and Great-Grandmother Nagyi were caught in the middle of a bloody battle.

"The bad news was that this was just the time when there were bombardments of Budapest. Budapest was still under Nazi control and the Russians started to bombard Budapest, and there were, literally, these huge bombs that would destroy entire buildings. We were hiding in one what would be described today as a massive condo. Other Jews were hiding with us, but most were not, and food was very scarce."

I didn't need to go far to imagine what this was like. Ukraine was under the same sort of attack right now.

"Once the bombardments began en masse, we all were forced to move into the basement for our own safety to avoid the bombs. We had to sleep four people in a bed because there was no space. And the people in the building were very suspicious of us. 'Who were we?' they wondered. There was a palpable paranoia in the air."

Could it be possible that some of these people who surrounded my mom survived too? And could any of them still be alive? I knew it was a question I'd never learn the answer to.

"Suddenly and frighteningly, we were forced into the public eye. This is when spending so much time in the Catholic school came in handy. I had learned the 'Our Father' and our Christian prayers. I had a good memory and a strong voice, and I would belt out the prayers so others would think we were not Jewish."

To this day, my mom knows those same Christian prayers. They must've been heard because how else could you explain her presence here today?

"I would kneel next to the bed and say these prayers in a very loud voice every night."

During her escape and subsequent hiding, my mom learned a tough lesson way too early in life: mistakes could be deadly.

"Our false documents all had different names from our actual ones. Never once did I slip up and call my mother by the wrong name. I told you I was a smart little girl. I became the de facto hero of my family."

Confidence and assertiveness are as much a part of my mom as her light-brown eyes and reddish-brown hair. She needed both to survive.

"My mother and grandmother and the others hiding claimed I saved them."

Trapped in Budapest in 1945 as people tiptoed around bombs and bodies in the streets, concerns only grew with food becoming scarce and the Russians advancing into the city's center.

"My mother, who later in life became a hypochondriac and worrier, found incredible strength during these bombardments.

She was our leader. After bombings, she would go into the streets with a big kitchen knife. At that time, horse and buggy was still the primary way we got around. Dead horses littered the streets. They were collateral damage of the bombings. My mother would take that kitchen knife and slice off pieces of the horse, which we would cook and eat. It was our only food. Our only way to stay nourished."

My Grandma Anyu didn't speak any English, so we only ever spoke through gestures and head nods. She always looked somewhat sad, like she'd seen the worst side of humanity, which she, in fact, had.

"My mother was very brave in so many other ways. She refused to leave me behind, for example, when she went out to get flour. We would see people being killed by the Russians, one dropping while another ran. But she was tough as nails and just trying to survive in a rough world."

My mom has a slew of sayings, which I'll get into later in this book, but she'd always tell us as kids, and now later in life, "We are all just trying to survive in a rough world." I pitched it to her as the tagline for our podcast, and it stuck as stubbornly as her Hungarian accent.

"Eventually the Russians liberated Budapest from Nazi control. They had raped and murdered plenty of innocents in the process but spared my mother and grandmother because they spoke a Cyrillic language like the Russians."

I had never been a big fan of history. Now I realized exactly why it was so important seeing it repeat itself, right now, in Kyiv.

"There was a rumor that the Russians were getting closer and closer and closer. By this time, they were fighting for close to six straight years. Soldiers were away from their families.

They had become wild and crazy. The Russians invaded and would see these young women. Right away, they took them to another little basement area and raped them. We heard the women scream as they shot the men in their head. They hated the Hungarians because they put up a resistance."

Although my mom was from Yugoslavia, now Serbia, her first language was Hungarian. She feared something as simple as her accent could cost her life.

"When they finally reached our building, my mother purposely wore a black scarf on her head, and she went over to an officer and said in Serbian, which is a little bit like Russian, a Slavic language, and said to him, 'Please help us. We are from Yugoslavia. We are refugees here.'"

This was like listening to a macabre version of *Harry Potter*, just as fantastical to me. But it was true. Did my own mom and grandmother really do all this to survive?

"Unbelievably, the officer my mother approached was Jewish. And, so, he really helped my mother. He didn't rape her. He was very civilized. He was very helpful. He protected us. He got us food. I remember he even got me some chocolate."

PART SEVEN: THE LONG STRANGE TRIP HOME

It was time for my mom's long, strange trip back home.

"It was a two-hour train ride back to Subotica. But, because of all the bombings and warfare, the tracks were destroyed, and there was no train to be had. So, we wrapped our few belongings in blankets and slung them over our shoulders. We began to walk."

As if the pain of the war wasn't brutal enough, now my mom, grandmother, and great-grandmother had to muster up the energy for a days-long walk.

"When the blankets became too heavy to carry, we simply dragged them through the snow on the road. It was March, so it was still really cold and gray. What should've taken us two hours by train took two long weeks in horrendous conditions."

And, when they finally made it all the way back, it was far from anything resembling home, sweet home. In fact, the sweetness turned into sorrow and bitterness.

"When we finally arrived back in Subotica, the locals greeted us beautifully. They were very warm, nice, and helpful. While everything was seemingly destroyed by the war, somehow, Subotica remained unscathed. It was like nothing happened."

My mom told me she found this even more disturbing. It was like time had stopped just before the madness began swirling all around them.

"The Jewish community quickly organized. There was something like eight thousand Jews before the war of which roughly only one thousand survived. Of those who survived, about eight hundred immigrated to Israel, which was just forming as a state. So, that left us with only a couple of hundred Jews. It was eerily quiet and empty. It was just so empty. The silence was only interrupted by my mother's crying. She sobbed and wailed for my dad and her own father who were both gassed in Auschwitz."

They were back home, but all the warmth of the place they once loved was gone in what seemed like an instant. And the worst part? There was nowhere else to go, no escape.

"We moved back into our home that was built by my father's father, your great-grandfather. He built it especially for my mother and father when they were married. So, this was truly their house. Through all the tears and loss, we picked up the pieces and kept living in our home."

Actual Voicemail from My Mom: May 9, 2022

Jo-el,

I'd like to know if you were thinking of coming here this afternoon because I'm going to the beach with...with... with....um...with Sarah.

And, um, if I knew, I'd prepare snacks beforehand.

Okay, I'll ask you, I mean, I'll write to you, I mean I'll text. You know what I mean.

Okay, it's your mother.

Your father is doing okay today.

"I RECOMMEND A GOOD MARRIAGE"

My mom's cell phone began ringing. She keeps it on a strap over her shoulder, and when she went to answer, she unknowingly held it to her head upside down.

"I can't hear you!" she agitatedly informed the person on the other end.

"You're speaking into the earpiece," I told her as I digested her sad but stunning story of survival.

"What?" she asked.

Now there was also drilling above us. I couldn't even enjoy my moment of sorrow after hearing my mother's story. I wanted to sulk for a moment in peace and, of course, in quiet too. First, a balcony repairman appeared and disrupted our conversation. I never anticipated that a mysterious driller lurking a floor or two above us would rattle us once again just mere moments later.

"What the hell is going on here?" I wondered aloud. "This is a nice building. How could so much need such improving all at once?"

"Hello?" my mom bellowed into the phone again.

"Turn it around. Turn it the other way; it's upside down," I explained.

"What? I can't hear you because of the drilling."

I grabbed her cell and turned it around the right way for her.

"That's not good," my mom said, speaking even louder than usual because of the din of the drill. I knew right away that someone from Miami Jewish, my dad's nursing home, was on the other end of this very disjointed call.

"His hemoglobin is six point three?" my mom asked, obviously repeating what she was just told. "What's it supposed to be?"

She spoke for another minute or so and then hung up.

"Your father isn't well. I think this may be the end," she told me. "His hemoglobin is supposed to be above eight, and he will need a transfusion."

Between the survival story I just intently listened to and my mom's almost daily declarations of my dad's imminent demise, I felt sad and emotional. I'd always joked with my parents about not knowing how to continue in life without them, but now, this once far-removed thought was inching closer to reality.

I stared through the sliding glass door and noticed the balcony repairman's cables were still in place, wondering if he'd come back too, just to balance out the driller.

"Think he's coming back?" I asked her.

"Who?"

"Balcony repairman."

"Why don't you focus? Why don't you focus on what we are doing instead of digressing already?"

With my book deadline looming, my mom knew I wanted to speak to her about another subject today: marriage.

It was my idea to share her perspective on Life with a capital "L." She'd been through so much and also trained as a professional therapist, so I knew her wisdom could help others.

With my dad's health condition worsening, I felt increasing pressure to get my mom on the proverbial record before it became too late.

We recorded this conversation as we did so many others over the weeks and days it took to put this all together. I was further motivated by almost daily headlines of Holocaust survivors dying from old age. My mom was a young eighty-four, if such a thing is possible, but I still felt that unnerving pressure of the passing of time. Before our podcast pivoted to true crime, we once interviewed Carole Baskin of *Tiger King* fame. She said something that stuck with me. My mom was an endangered species just like tigers. Holocaust survivors were leaving us in droves and would soon all be gone. There was no more time to waste in sharing my mom—and her story—something I'd always wanted to do but had always successfully procrastinated in accomplishing. Now, reality smacked me in the face.

"Marriage. Is it something you would recommend?" I blurted out.

"Yes." We both laughed because she didn't hesitate for a second.

"And, how come? Expound. Don't just give me one-word answers. It will make for a magazine article, not a book."

My mom set her phone down on the coffee table. I noticed she had enabled voice messaging, and she was mistakenly going to text some unlucky person our entire conversation.

"I swear I didn't do it on purpose. That's funny. Modern times you can't trust your phone even. It's spying on us."

I was about to ask my mom something I had never wondered about until right now. "Were your parents happily married?"

After World War Two, Grandma Anyu remarried. Her second husband was named Laszlo Senes, the same first name as my grandfather who was gassed in Auschwitz. In fact, my second daughter is named Zizi, combining the letter "z" from each of my grandfathers. I tell her frequently that she has the most meaningful name in our entire family. It was only when she was around three years old that I discovered Zizi also means "penis" in French. When we visited Paris over the summer it got super awkward.

"As a child, I was witness to a pretty lousy marriage," my mom said, dropping a dose of reality on me that I had never known before. She was staring at my Starbucks iced venti green tea.

"Are you out of your zombie mind? Don't spill it on my new rug!" she screamed. I didn't think it was possible for my mom to become more excitable. But, between the stress of dealing with my dad and her increasing age, her shrieking became even more commonplace.

"My stepfather, your grandfather, died of Parkinson's at sixty-six. We found his journal, and it was one of the most painful things. I tried to avoid it, but it was too late. He never fell out of love with his first wife and child who were both gassed in Auschwitz. He described her as the "girl of his dreams." It turns out they were going to have a second child together too. She was pregnant when she was gassed. He eventually married Grandma Anyu, but he admitted in this journal that he never loved her the same way. I don't know why, but it was very hurtful."

A Bank of America alert suddenly popped up on my phone. Quite possibly, the only thing that had the ability to elevate my blood pressure more than my mom's voice was a bank or money issue.

"What are you looking at?" my mom wanted to know.

"My bank account, and it's not pretty," I told her. She knew I was obsessively and irrationally worried about finances. My dad was born into the Great Depression, and I think I inherited his financial trauma. As a by-product of the Great Depression and Holocaust, the odds were always stacked against me to maintain any semblance of normalcy.

"I literally cannot stop worrying about money," I confessed for the umpteenth time.

"I can't cure stupidity," she said. "Neurotic people like you are exhausting. They wear out other people. Do you want to know my thoughts about marriage or not? Your father is much smarter and more interesting than me, so why don't you just write a book about him?"

"Did Grandma Anyu ever read Laszlo Two's diary?" I asked.

"My mother not only read it, but she also wrote an introduction to it and self-published it. Laszlo Two was a very depressed, very wounded person after the war. And, because of that, my own mother being a pain in the ass, they had a lousy marriage. They were old school, and they had their loyalties to each other, but passion? There was very little."

"This is unbelievable. He's back. Turn around," I said.

Incredibly, the balcony repairman once again appeared before us as he descended downward.

"He's going down. Obviously, he's going down for lunch." My mom didn't miss a beat. "They had fights about silly things, and my mother would storm away. I was a very precocious young girl, and I would say very openly, 'If you two get divorced, I'm going with my father.'"

My mom's cell phone rang at a decibel level I didn't think was possible for an iPhone. I looked over. Charlotte Schwartz's name popped up on the screen. I glared at her, and my mom silenced the call.

"What would they argue about?"

"That he's ignoring her. He's paying too much attention to his two siblings and that he doesn't care about her."

It's amazing, I thought to myself, that people have been miserably married since the beginning of time. It was just part of the human condition.

"Your grandmother even thought he was cheating on her!"

"I remember him as being pretty ugly," I said. Laszlo Two died when I was just seven years old.

"He was ugly. But he said a man must only be one shade less ugly than the devil to get a woman. He wasn't that ugly really. He was bald with eyeglasses. He was brilliant. He was very smart. He was a very warm person. And he had a great sense of humor. What else do you need? But I grew up with this notion of marriage that it's not great."

After hearing all this, I was confused. "So, why do you recommend marriage?"

"I recommend a *good* marriage."

We were so engrossed in our conversation that we had completely tuned out the person drilling a few floors above, until he apparently hit a piece of metal, which jolted my heart rate back up.

"Roy, your father, experienced the same kind of marriage. His parents had a difficult relationship. Grandpa Milton couldn't make a living. And your Grandma Helen was very temperamental and annoying."

It made me wonder: Were my mom and dad happily married for more than sixty-three years? It certainly seemed like they were.

"If you and Dad both grew up as children of difficult marriages, why do you think yours has succeeded so well for seven decades?"

"It's impossible to sum up our relationship in just a few words. First, we had a magnetic, physical attraction from day one. We wanted to touch; we wanted to hold each other; we wanted to be close; we wanted to make love. He maybe a little more frequently than me, but we both wanted the same thing."

Anytime you hear parents and lovemaking in the same sentence, it's a good time to change the subject. But I figured I'd double down.

"Do you still do it?"

"I'm not kidding you. I reviewed my journal the other day and in 2020, it was still going on, but less frequently. But the physical part is still there. I know it's hard for you to understand this."

"What do you think Dad found physically attractive about you?"

My mom stared at me. She was in her robe with her glasses on her head. Her ankles were swollen from walking around too much earlier in the day. I thought it was a fair question. Her compression socks looked worn and slightly frayed. The staring contest continued for a few more moments, and then she cracked a smile.

"That is the sixty-four-thousand-dollar question." She laughed. "Because I am flabby, fat with short legs and a big mouth."

My parents first met while my dad was a medical student at the University of Geneva, and my mom was an undergrad there. They locked eyes one random weeknight while listening to a speech at the Maison Juive, or "Jewish house," on campus.

"We also had a meaningful relationship where we communicated about everything. We didn't hide anything from each other. We spoke openly. More than the physical attraction was our desire to listen to each other. We truly cared about each other."

"How long did you date before he proposed?"

"Today, everything is performative. It's for show, for Instagram, for the rest of the world to see. We didn't need to rent an airplane and fly it over Miami Beach. Your father didn't even have money for a ring, and I never even expected one."

"Did he get down on one knee?"

When I proposed to my wife, Ileana, at the fancy Daniel Restaurant in Manhattan, I was so nervous that I forgot my wallet. I had no choice but to call my mom who bailed me out by giving the maitre d' her credit card. It was an inauspicious start.

"Your dad absolutely did not get down on one knee. He had a bad knee anyway. I was only twenty-one at the time, and I kept telling him I was too young to get married. He accepted it and then sort of forgot about it."

"About asking you to marry him?" Sounded about right for my dad who could get deeply lost in his own thoughts.

"He left for Israel for a few months. He came back and then I asked him after a lovemaking session, which I remember, I said to him, 'By the way, do you still plan to marry me?' He said, 'Yes.' So, it was really me who asked for your father's hand in marriage."

Now I was sort of ashamed I actually asked my wife to marry me instead of the baller move my dad had pulled. He was always unintentionally very cool. I had never known any of this, by the way.

"And your wedding was small, right?"

"It was your Grandma Helen who sealed the deal because, being the symbol of virtue, she didn't want us sleeping in the same bed in her home. So, I said, 'What the hell, I'll get married now.'"

Being the shallow human being I am, I was still fixated on the engagement ring, or lack thereof. "At any point did Dad give you an engagement ring prior to your wedding?"

"Yes, ten years after we were married. A decade later, he finally had enough money."

After my own wedding, we honeymooned in Rwanda and Tanzania. It was always my dream to see gorillas and animals on a safari in their natural element. During a cab ride in Kigali, the driver hesitantly asked why Ileana was wearing a diamond on her finger. He couldn't fathom why anyone would want a ring and not a goat, which is tradition in Rwanda, because it provides milk for an entire family. He made a great point, and I began to wonder how many goats, ergo quarts of milk I could've squeezed out of the diamond now pointlessly sitting on my bride's finger.

Something else suddenly occurred to me. Is anyone reading this going to care about any of it?

"Is anyone going to give a shit about this story?"

"You're an idiot. This is for you. This is so you have a book to accompany our podcast, and so you know something about your own family—so you're not a hollow head. Maybe it will enlighten others. Maybe it won't. But please don't be stupid and other-oriented. What's your father always tell you? Mind your business!"

My parents eventually tied the knot on July 25, 1961. It's a date even I could never screw up because yours truly was born on their anniversary eight years later in 1969. I'd like to think I was the best gift they ever received, but it's up for debate according to many others.

"Twenty-four people were at our wedding. Nobody from my side of the family. My own mother wasn't there because she couldn't leave Yugoslavia."

"Did you feel bad?" I asked already knowing the answer. My mom never second-guessed a decision and certainly never exerted what she perceived as wasted emotion once she had decided upon something.

"I remember I didn't feel bad because I thought marriage is like just a formality. It's nothing."

My mom survived so much partly because she never let her feelings derail her from what she needed to do.

Just as she was speaking, I waded back into exactly what my mom was so good at avoiding: emotion. "I'm going to have an aneurysm from the stress of this book. It's just weighs on me so much, trying to get it right."

"Say once more you will have an aneurysm, and you *will* have an aneurysm. You will will it." My mom was used to my intermittent non sequiturs. "You deserve one, moron," she added petulantly.

"Okay, so you get married in Grandma Helen's house with twenty-four people crammed in their Long Beach, New York, home?"

"Yes, we borrowed chairs, we borrowed chairs from neighbors. And I remember your great aunt Simi, who ice skated until she was eighty-eight years old, came even though she was a recent widow. Her husband died of throat cancer."

Growing up, it always amazed me how much the Jewish people I knew would find ways to seamlessly interject how people either died or were gravely ill. It impacted me so much that when we first launched our *Surviving the Survivor* podcast, I insisted on a segment entitled "This Week in Dead and Dying."

"Do you want to tell me how anyone else's spouses from your wedding died?" My mom laughed, realizing the absurdity.

"In the living room we were married in, there was a green, shiny couch. It was a big living room. It had a piano; it had a fireplace."

"Comparable to the Bacara where I was married?" My wife and I tied the knot at an upscale Santa Barbara resort. It was a destination wedding, and now I was embarrassed, wondering what our Kigali cab driver would have thought. The same one who couldn't negotiate in his own mind why on earth my wife would prefer a diamond ring over a goat.

"Yes, it was similar. Very similar to the bathroom at the Bacara. Anyway, we had a chuppah, which was Rabbi Hillel Clavin's tallit, better known as his prayer shawl. After we folded his tallit, we unfolded twenty-four chairs, and all ate lunch. That was our lavish wedding," my mom sarcastically added.

"How much did your wedding cost?"

"I would say a couple of hundred dollars."

I could see our Kigali cab driver's face beaming with pride.

"Now that you've had sixty-three years to reflect, what do you think made your marriage work?"

"One of the things that made it work is a miracle. It's a miracle. The second thing that made it work is that we both decided we don't want the marriages our parents had. And we don't want negativity in our lives. I know you don't believe this. And we really worked on that part too."

"Was it a conscious decision?"

"Yes. Our parents, as I just told you, had bad marriages. And we told ourselves we are going to have a good one. We spoke openly about it."

"I think most people who grow up in bad marriages replicate their parents' marriages. Why do you think you were able to create a different sort of dynamic?"

"It's a very good question."

Wow, a compliment from my mom. Those were earned.

"I think it was because of this attraction and because your dad is a very nice person. He is always the more accepting, loving, less stubborn one. He is no pushover, but he is never difficult like me."

There was a running joke in our family that wasn't really a joke. It was our reality and, more importantly, my father's. There was rarely a day that passed without my mom yelling at my dad for something.

"Like you said, I've never had a day without yelling at him. But I yell at him with a lot of love. It's all from my heart because I care."

My wife must've learned from my mom, I thought to myself.

"Why did you yell at him every day?"

"He frustrated me. He would not do something exactly the way I imagined he should do it. No, no, really? I really love the guy. That's all I can say. I yell because I love him, and I'm not that normal."

"What would you say was the most difficult stretch of your marriage?"

"There's no question it's when he promised we would move to Israel. He kept his promise, and we lived there. But, after only three years, he insisted on moving back here because he couldn't make money as a doctor in Israel."

"So, it wasn't the loss of your child?"

"No."

"Making you leave Israel was worse than losing your child?" I asked not being able to fully grasp her answer. I had my own children now and knew I'd never fully recover if something, God forbid, happened to one of them. My mom clarified what she was telling me.

"Losing the baby was worse for me emotionally. But leaving Israel was more taxing on our marriage. You wouldn't be here if losing a child stopped us."

During the editing of this book, the war broke out in Israel after the worst single loss of Jewish lives since the Holocaust. Reports began to circulate about Hamas beheading babies, and I could see the pain and despair on my mother's face.

"Not even the Nazis did this," she told me.

We had lived in Tel Aviv during the Yom Kippur War, and I still held on to very vague memories of Israeli Air Force jets zipping up and down the Mediterranean coast rattling our windows.

"I'm so worried about Joe and Yaron, I'm sick. I never thought I'd see it this bad again. What happened to 'Never Again'?" my mom asked rhetorically.

Joe and Yaron, both infantrymen and elite members of the IDF's Paratrooper Unit, were called up as reservists. They were preparing for battle on the Lebanon border. They are both my nephews through marriage.

War in Israel was the singular subject I knew could not be joked about with my mom. Even though she no longer lived there, it's the only place she's ever really considered home.

"Why was it so hard for you that Dad wanted to leave Israel?"

My mom immediately got emotional. Her eyes got wet and red. She dabbed them with a Kleenex.

"This is very emotional for me. I felt that after all that happened, and was now incredibly happening again, that Israel is where I belonged. It was always my life plan to live there. After my father was gassed in Auschwitz, I made this promise to myself and I felt, by leaving, I was betraying that vow.

"This war might be the end of me. I'm just so stressed out," she told me, fiddling with her neck. "I'm not even sure what I did with my Life Alert. Have you seen it?"

Yes, that Life Alert. The "help me I can't get up" one. Since my dad was so ill in the hospital my sister and I insisted she wear it in case she slipped and, you guessed it, couldn't get up. The advertising worked on us.

"I don't know what I did with it," my mom admitted sheepishly.

She sat for a moment. Nothing could tug at my mom's heartstrings, besides her own children, like her other child: Israel. She watched its birth in 1948 when so many Holocaust survivors fled there for safety and comfort.

My mom could never stay depressed or serious more than a few minutes. It just wasn't part of her fabric, even during the worst moments. She cracked a half smile.

"On the other hand, if I'm being totally honest, I didn't like being poor either. Your father was traumatized by the superintendent always knocking on the door of his childhood apartment asking for the rent. He didn't only become a doctor to help people, but also because it was a profession you could make money with those days. It's different now with our screwed-up health-care system. But, in Israel, it was always difficult to make money as a physician because it's socialized medicine."

"Do you think that's why I'm so tense about money?" I asked knowing full well the response that was coming my way.

"I'm not talking about you. The hell with you!" My mom hated when I interjected myself and, worse, my feelings about certain things. I always know it'll elicit a sharp reaction. She's easy to bait in that way.

"If leaving Israel was the most difficult time, what was the best part of your marriage?"

"The best part of our marriage, the way I remember it, was just being able to live a very comfortable, middle-class existence. It wasn't one thing."

My parents raised us in Highland Park, New Jersey, a stone's throw from Rutgers University, where many of my friends' parents were professors. It was a great place to grow up with smart, good people. On our podcast set I proudly keep a small New Jersey flag and a hat with the name of my hometown. I'm *that* guy who buys Jersey shirts every time I land at Newark Liberty.

"People look to you for advice—"

My mom immediately interrupted me.

"No one should look to me for anything. What do I know? Because I'm a Holocaust survivor? Because I lost a child? Because I have wrinkles now? I know less than most."

My mom had begun to feel the burden of being a dwindling number of Holocaust survivors. In recent years, it both amazed and troubled her that people would ask her for blessings *just* because she survived a horrific time in world history. She felt she just got lucky. I tried to appease her.

"Okay, I get it, you don't know anything. But, if someone hypothetically asked, what would you tell them is the key to a successful marriage?"

"I never idealized anything. I never made something bigger than it was. I just always looked forward to going to bed with your father every night, and I'm not talking about sex. I miss him so much now that he's in Miami Jewish. We would hug or just talk. He was a very calming, reassuring voice."

I wondered if my mom would ever have this chance again. It was doubtful. My dad was close to ninety, and his physical health was just getting worse, it seemed. I became sad thinking how true it is that all good things must eventually come to an end. But how could such love be extinguished? Maybe it never would be. Something just didn't feel fair or right.

"A successful marriage comes down to this: Firstly, you have to find somebody who will put up with your crap. Secondly, you can both have issues and be neurotic, but it should be about different things. Avoid having the same neuroses. You should complement each other. For example, your father was anxious about money. Meanwhile, I was totally oblivious to money because I knew he was financially savvy. To me, money was like monopoly money."

I was beginning to wonder if my own wife was somehow biologically related to my mom. Both liked to yell, neither worried about money...

"My mother always said, 'If it's a money problem, it's not a problem.' I was never anxious about money. We reassured each other. We used to joke with each other that we had such a good life if only we could afford it. Anyway, marriage is a delicate balance."

"You once told me, and I forget exactly, but you said that marriage is like a balance of power. What did you mean by that?"

"Let's say you put fifty on this side and fifty on this side. It stays in balance. In marriage, sometimes it's sixty-forty. It gets very dangerous if it's one hundred percent on one side in terms of giving and doing everything. That means the other spouse is doing nothing. It must be a somewhat equal balance."

Speaking of balance, the drilling overhead began again, and we had to speak louder to offset the disquieting sounds reverberating in my mom's condo once more.

"I think empathy is also a very important thing in marriage. Trying to put yourself into the other person's position. I admittedly wasn't great at this myself. But you must put yourself in the position of the other person and understand where the other person is coming from."

Growing up the son of two therapists, people would always jokingly ask me if I was crazy. And the answer, of course, is yes, sort of. You learn grown-up words like "anxiety" and "depression" much earlier in life than your friends. And your parents' friends are invariably in the same business. Zvi Lothane has been a practicing psychiatrist for close to sixty years and friends with my mom and dad even longer. He speaks nine languages fluently, has an office on Lexington Avenue that is straight out of a movie, and even once owned a German shepherd, (to the dismay of my mother, who still refuses to buy products from Hitler's homeland) named Sigmund Freud. He has always epitomized to me the zaniness often associated with the psychology field.

"How did Zvi once define marriage to you?" I asked my mom.

"He once asked me, which I remember very well, 'Do you know the definition of psychotherapy?' He answered his own question, saying, 'It means you talk about pee-pee, ka-ka, your mama and papa."

"What's that have to do with marriage?"

"Patience, young child, I'm getting there."

The drilling stopped. Again. Neither of us even really noticed or cared anymore.

"He then asked, 'Do you know the definition of marriage?' Again, it was a rhetorical question. He answered, 'It's who will bury whom.'"

This is precisely why kids of therapists like yours truly cannot escape their childhoods unscathed. We're exposed to macabre humor way too early in life.

"I remember joking with Zvi, telling him I prefer to die simultaneously with your father."

Not surprisingly, I didn't find this funny. It triggered a memory of my dad always sharing *New Yorker* cartoons with me. He'd belly laugh, and I would never think they were funny either.

"When you come to the end, usually one person has to bury the other one. It's the not-so-happy ending of a marriage and life. It's implied it's the very best outcome. If it ends any other way, your marriage likely wasn't a successful one."

This part of the conversation strangely reminded me of the time my uncle Ron, who to his credit helped eradicate small-pox in the 1970s, also markedly affected my level of insecurity when he mocked me for not knowing what angst meant. I was seven years old. Everyone at the Passover Seder table that year laughed. I felt like the proverbial "Simple Son," which has sort of lasted a lifetime.

"Marriage is, quite possibly, the most important decision of one's life. The other person helps mold and define you, no matter what level of independence you think you have. Your father is never critical of me. Maybe that's why I'm so obnoxious. After a certain amount of time, you begin to think, *Maybe I am perfect.*"

"There's plenty to criticize," I joked. My mom and I knew there was an element of truth to what I was saying. Few people call my mom out because she's such a force of nature—except me. I'm the one who always keeps her in check.

"Your father built me up and never tore me down. He helped give me the confidence to be me. My mother did very much the same."

"Wow, Grandma Anyu sounds just like you," I joked again. "I had no idea she wasn't critical of you. I always just assumed she was very tough on you. Why are you so hard on me?" I asked.

She ignored the question.

"Marriage is, hands down, the most important decision of your life. And we usually make it when we're not prepared for it. We're usually young and naïve."

Maybe this is why I waited until forty-one to propose to Ileana. I still joke with my mom that I'm worried I got married way too young. No one thought it would ever happen.

"And so much of it is either good or bad luck, you know? A bad decision can consume you and ruin your life. Luckily, there's divorce. You know divorce is part of the Jewish religion. We're a very practical people. Sometimes you just make a mistake, and it needs to be fixed."

"There's a growing trend of young people choosing not to get married. What do you think of this?"

"I think they're making a tremendous mistake. But not because they're not getting married. Because they're not having children!"

Actual Voicemail from My Mom: *June 8, 2022*

Hi Jo-el and family.

How are you? Vida and hopefully Zizi are okay and hopefully Judah is okay, and hopefully you're all okay.

Okay, let me know.

I have spaghetti and cut-up watermelon for everyone. Your kids think I make the best fruit, and I don't want to destroy the illusion.

Love Mom and Grandma.

"I'M PRO-CHILDREN"

Around Yom HaShoah, better known to most as Holocaust Remembrance Day, Karm is in higher demand than most other days. *Tiger King*'s Carole Baskin's remark on our podcast that my mom's an endangered species is never more evident than on this sad day. Media outlets and Jewish organizations from all over call weeks, if not months, in advance, hoping she'll speak to them. They always cite the ever-increasing decrease of survivors.

This past year, she spoke at Hebrew Academy, a prominent Miami Beach school. My kids accompanied her, and I couldn't help but shed a tear myself because it's one of the few times I felt like I made a significant contribution in my life. I mean, what's our purpose here on this planet?

In that moment, I knew my children were my purpose. It's the first time I ever felt this. I was rarely certain, but I was sure Vida, Zizi, and Judah Mac, named for the famous warrior of the Jewish people, would be my legacy. I'm also admittedly a guy who likes to hold a grudge. And there's no group of people I loathe, abhor, and despise more than the Nazis who tried to destroy my family, my religion, and Jews' identity. My children are payback for killing my grandfather and 5,999,999 million others. They're living proof that we're not dying off anytime soon.

"Last time we spoke, you seemed okay with people choosing not to get married. But you say you feel badly for people who don't have children. Why do you think it is so important to have children?" I continued my line of questioning.

"I really thought from a young age that this is one of the wonderful things that life offers. I could never relate to people willingly choosing not to have children. Even while getting my master's in social work, I would openly tell people that I'm biased. I'm pro-marriage and pro-children. I could care less if you're gay, lesbian, or an alien from Mars. I still think everyone should experience the joy of parenthood. And, if for some reason, you can't have children on your own, then adopt. So many children need a loving home."

"Why do you think you felt this way at such a young age?"

"Like it or not, girls are taught to play with dolls. I remember styling my doll's hair in Subotica. Now, I watch your son who plays with building blocks and cars. He runs around screaming, 'Zoom zoom.'"

"It's vroom, vroom. Zoom is for conference calls." I always got a demented pleasure from correcting my mom's aphorisms, which she still struggles with to this day, as you can see.

"Whatever. Who cares? Do you want to hear my take or correct my English?"

"Please continue."

"He screams vroom, vroom. He wrestles other kids, including his sisters. His sisters' rooms are filled with dolls. Us girls are maternal from a very young age. It's in our DNA. Let me tell you what happened yesterday—"

"Please stick to the subject. You're not the one who has to go back and transcribe all these conversations and then write the book."

"I don't give a shit. I'm going to tell you about yesterday. Why don't you ever hear other people's stories? Don't be a self-centered asshole!"

This was a common refrain from my mom. I admit it; sometimes I am selfish and self-centered. But I happen to be on a book deadline too. As a broadcast news journalist, I was always serious about meeting those deadlines. But this was going to be different because it involved my mom.

"Yesterday was Israel's memorial day for the victims of all the wars and acts of terrorism."

"Stick to the subject."

"No, I am not sticking to the subject!"

My mom hates being told what to do. She was forced to hide so she could survive, and since then she's never allowed others to compel her to do anything, including me.

"At this memorial day event, a thirty-seven-year-old man told a crazy story about his family's Passover holiday several years ago. The Seder was at a seaside resort in Israel, and he was a chain smoker, so he went outside for a few minutes to have a cigarette. Something caught his eye, he explained, and the next second there was a massive explosion in the banquet hall. Both his parents, in an instant, were blown to bits, along with his grandparents who were survivors."

"Can you imagine surviving the Holocaust only to be killed in a terrorist attack?" I asked rhetorically, always marveling at life's absurdities. "Do you know Matt Brode's grandpa, Papa Henry, survived but was struck by a car and killed in his late nineties at his lake house in northern Michigan?"

"Now you're interrupting with your usual stupidity. Do you want me to continue?"

I gave her the affirmative head nod. She hated when I mentioned Matt Brode, a close friend who forecasts weather for a living in Tucson, where it's sunny 363 days a year. He's also the son of a psychiatrist, and the two of us have a slight tendency to dwell on our anxieties, thereby making them significantly worse. It's fun in a twisted way. I could tell my mom was irritated, which also brought me some joy, if I'm being completely honest.

"This man's only sister arrived a few moments later. She was late, and it saved her life. A cigarette saved his. We never know when it's our time."

"What does this have to do with children? We're discussing children."

"I'll tell you, asshole."

"I'm putting this in the book. You know that, right? I'm recording these conversations."

"Don't you dare put that in," my mom laughed. "People think I'm this sweet old lady who blesses people by the pool."

"Does your story have anything to do with children?"

"He was asked how many children he has, and he answered six. He had a child for each of the six relatives, including his grandparents, that he lost in that terror attack."

Now it was starting to make sense.

"That may be the answer as to why I wanted children so badly and so early in my life. I lost a lot too suddenly. So, that's my response."

I looked down at the screensaver of my kids on my iPhone. I felt like a bit of a schmuck.

"Even at a young age, I knew I had to make up for all the losses we experienced. Grandma Anyu was having trouble conceiving with Laszlo Two, and he was devastated because he lost his only son in the war. When she was finally able to get pregnant, they were so happy. She was born the same year Israel became a country in 1948."

My mom began to veer off on a tangent about her sister. This time I knew I had to rein her in for your sake so this book could be read in under a year. It was beginning to feel like I was chronicling the oral history of the Jews. This isn't supposed to be a modern-day version of the Talmud. My redirect was swift and firm.

"Did you think that I would ever have children?" It was a question I knew would trigger my mom with the exact answer I was expecting.

"It's not about you! It's not about you!"

"Did you think I'd have kids?"

"No, I did not think you would have children. I definitely didn't think you would have children. But I was very happy when you did. I'm not even sure when you decided to have them. I always knew you would make a fantastic father. You were always too busy getting ready for life instead of being involved with life."

It was a compliment. But it was also an underhanded insult. I've never known anyone better at executing the "comp-insult" than my mom.

"Do you wish that you had more children?" I asked.

"My fantasy when I was a child was always to have four sons."

"Why?"

"I thought four was a good number. I wanted powerful, strong sons. Brave sons." *She hit the jackpot with me*, I thought. The other day I noticed a raised mole on my back and saw my life flash before my eyes.

"Why not daughters?"

"Because in my head I was fighting still. I was looking for warriors to help fight with me."

"I'm tough," I said sheepishly. My phone began blowing up with alerts. "Holy shit, Don Lemon was fired from CNN! Can you believe this?"

"Don Lemon doesn't exist in my world!"

"He does in mine. What a great day! Fuck these guys with their crazy egos!"

The news business is as cutthroat as they come. People gaze into your eyes as they drive the knife as deep into your back as they can. Over the years it made me angry, which I found a strangely strong motivator.

"News is a game like Chutes and Ladders. Remember it?" my mom reminded me. "One minute you're on top, the next you've slid to the bottom. Worry about yourself! Don Lemon shouldn't exist in your world, I said!"

I got up and did a quick happy dance. My mom shook her head in disgust. Her patience was running thin, so I got back to the questions, "So you wanted children because of the loss you experienced. Why should someone who has not experienced your level of trauma want to have children?"

"I think children are wonderful. They are not corrupted yet. They are still open-minded. They are still in awe of everything. Everything is new to them. Everything is beautiful to them. You know, they say from the mouth of babes comes the truth. They're like little teddy bears, you know? They're so huggable. They run around, and then need to be recharged. They are wonderful people. It's wonderful watching them develop."

"Fuck you, Don Lemon," I blurted out.

"Shut up, asshole, or I'm leaving. Grow up!"

The news business is replete with nepotism and nonsensical hires. Don Lemon as a major talent just never made any sense to me. He was getting twenty-five million dollars to leave CNN. The truth is I always wanted a job like Don Lemon's. I worked so hard to get there, but it wasn't to be. It took me years to achieve some sort of peace of mind with what I accomplished in that world. But I'd still never let anyone remove that chip off my shoulder. It still drives me now.

"Why do you think some people just choose to never have children?"

"Who knows? It could be they've experienced trauma like me. Obviously, that didn't keep me from having kids. It could just be they're too self-centered." My mom exaggerated her stare at me.

"Can it be selfishness?"

"One hundred percent it could be selfishness because you're not just getting something from a child, you have to put yourself into that child. It's a lot of work to raise good children. It's a lifelong commitment."

"Can the converse be true? That it's selfish to have children?"

"Yes. I didn't want to be alone in my old age. Now your dad is at Miami Jewish, and he's only getting worse. And you're here interviewing me for a book no one will read because I'm not that interesting!"

"Why do you always have to insult me?"

"I said, 'I am not that interesting.' Not you!"

"Do you really think no one will buy this? Do you know how hard I'm working on this?"

"No one ever promised you a rose garden."

"Say people will buy it!"

"No!"

We perpetually push each other's buttons, which is exhausting. But we wouldn't have it any other way.

"So, how else do you see having children as a selfish desire?"

"Well, I just told you part of the reason I wanted to have children so badly is so I wouldn't be all alone in old age. Even though I visit your father in Miami Jewish every day, one of the most depressing places on earth, by the way, he's already not with me at nights. It's a very difficult, lonely adjustment after being together more than sixty-three years. You're right here irritating me. But at least you're here. So, it's selfish. Once you have your own children, they're almost your property, in a way, maybe a poor term, but you have them, and they're yours. And they can comfort you. Or drive you crazy, like you do to me."

We stared each other down. The truth is our relationship is probably even a bit more twisted when it's just the two of us alone, with no audience, no cameras, and no podcast.

"I've seen so many people, almost daily, who should not be parents because they either don't have the mental disposition or the financial means to raise them right, or both. So, who should really have children?" I wanted to know.

"Life never ceases to amaze me. And one of the things that I've always found interesting is how many people become parents when they shouldn't. You don't need a PhD, which maybe you should. All you need is to sleep with someone and get their sperm."

Anytime the word "sperm" comes out of your mother's mouth you cringe, including me. It took me back to when I was thirteen furtively listening to Dr. Ruth's radio show under my sheets on Sunday nights, and she would repeatedly say spermatozoa. People have always compared Dr. Ruth's accent to my mom's.

"Getting or giving sperm is relatively easy, it seems, except for those who tend to want to have children the most. It's one of life's many cruelties. But if you're lucky enough to have children, it's a lifetime of commitment. And it's an absolute myth that everyone's a wonderful parent. We all know there are plenty of terrible people raising children. And this is a real shame."

"Do you need financial success first to be good parents?"

"Your father and I couldn't rub two pennies together when we had your sister."

"But that's not realistic. You know how much children cost. If you and Dad didn't help me, I'd be living in a shelter."

"That's because you and your wife, excuse me for saying this, spend like idiots."

Anytime my mom excused herself before insulting me, I knew a slew of more slights were headed my way. Her voice started rising.

"If you two weren't so concerned with image and trying to impress others you'd be fine. But you spend and spend. And then you complain about money. It's like the kid who killed his parents and then asked for clemency from the courts! Did you ever see your father or me spending money on stupidity?"

"Okay, okay, stick to the answers. Otherwise, this will be the length of the Bible. What about having money as a parent? Important?"

"Only if you cave into what others think of you." My mom loved to hammer her points home in the form of verbal onslaughts, and this was one of them. "I just told you that we had no money when we had your sister, Arden. Our population would be at risk of disappearing if people waited for financial security."

She stared at my brand-new shoes. "How much were those?"

"Don't worry about it."

"Then don't whine about money."

"Aside from having a lot of money," I said to annoy my mom, "what is the key to being a good parent and not just someone who raises a child?"

A picture from my niece Judi's wedding hung behind my mom. She got married at the height of the pandemic, and our entire family is in it. My three children, my sister's five daughters and their significant others, and my mother and my father, who was healthy at the time. We were all wearing COVID masks. It was a photo that our family generations from now would invariably ask about because it looked so surreal. My mom turned to look at it and then paused for a moment.

"You know, they say the proof of good parenting is how the next generation treats their own children. You and your sister are both great parents. As children? Your behavior is questionable."

She was still annoyed with me for the money digression.

"First, all the child development theories around parenting pointed to nurture. Then, it was nature, then it was nurture again. So, who really knows? The one thing I know for sure is children need love and positive reinforcement."

"I'm not sure you give me enough positive reinforcement and love."

"You're fifty-four, moron. I gave you enough for seventeen lifetimes. I'm retired now."

"What do I need to do to be a great—not good—parent?"

"It's all a myth. There's no such thing as being a perfect parent or raising a flawless child. Neither exist. There are so many more variables than just how the parent raises a child because each kid is born with idiosyncratic characteristics unique to that specific child. Look how different you and Arden are."

Arden graduated from Boston University's six-year medical program at twenty-three, got married, and had five children while I was trying to find my way in the world, both as a man and as a news reporter. It took me about twenty years longer than Arden to figure it out. And most days I still feel like I'm lost and searching for answers.

"Two siblings are never the same; they're like snowflakes. It's because you are not only getting genes from the mother and father but from their parents too. A lot of it is simply a genetic lottery. I mean, your child could have a physical ailment, God forbid, or a personality trait from the 1800s. Genetics is a big part."

"So, you don't think that there's a universal secret to successful parenting?"

"I just went over it. Are you listening? Or are you just lost in your own self-wallowing thoughts?" She continued, ironically, "It's all about being loving and caring. Children also need structure. You clearly didn't have enough of that."

My iPhone began blowing up. Could this news be real? Tucker Carlson was fired from my former employer Fox News the same day as Don Lemon. I hadn't been this excited since discovering my boy is left-handed like me.

"They fired Tucker Carlson too!" I exclaimed joyously.

"Who cares?"

"I do! Besides my children being born, this quite possibly could be the greatest day of my life!"

"I'm leaving!"

"It's your condo, Mom."

"Oh yeah, I forgot!" she said. We both laughed.

"I hope they suffocate in their own misery. Good riddance to two dipshits. Ahahaha," I cackled.

"Joel, my time is very limited. I refuse to waste my time on this stupidity. They don't exist in my world, and you're worse than either of them for letting them exist in yours. I obviously failed at parenting."

Who could be fired next? I wondered. Deaths usually come in threes, after all. I refocused my giddiness. "So what else strikes you as important about parenting?"

"There are different parenting trends every generation. In the nineteen fifties, fathers were basically invisible. Even your own dad was working all the time. Mothers were in charge of the house and of the children."

My dad was at his office from 7 a.m. until 10 p.m. The Great Depression scared him into working almost around the clock. I can't remember him ever missing a day of work because he was sick or otherwise.

"Today, couples say we are pregnant…"

"That drives me crazy…"

"Well, be crazy then. Now couples parent together. We also hear expressions like 'helicopter parenting' and 'free-range' kids, so trends change with the times."

"How would you parent me differently if you could do it all over again?"

"I think I did a perfect job, and I wouldn't change anything. All joking aside, I spoiled you rotten. You think life owes you something, but it doesn't owe you shit. I've also said, 'Nobody promised you a rose garden,' but either you never got it or never wanted to. You think you deserve to have Tucker Carlson's or Don Lemon's fame and fortune! Why?"

I shrugged my shoulders. "They say small kids, small problems and big kids, big problems. Do you ascribe to this?"

"Sort of. A small kid runs a fever. You still get all worked up. You run with her to the doctor. She usually gets medicine, and she's fine. When she's older, now the problems are much more complex, related to work or finances or romance, or worst case, it's health related. And as a parent you're older too and therefore more vulnerable. That's why I don't have time for your stupid bullshit, especially about Don Lemon or Tucker Carlson because, trust me, they have their own problems."

"Really, like what?" My eyes lit up.

"I knew this would make you happy. Life is never easy. Never be happy with other's failures."

I've always held on to anger as motivation. My mom who has so much reason to be angry never has and likely never will.

"What do you think of my children?"

"I think your wife, Ileana, is doing a terrific job raising them."

She knew this would get a rise out of me. And it did. But I also marveled at my mom's ability to drop verbal bombs so effortlessly.

For whatever reason, her comment took me back to a time when we were on a bus in Jerusalem years ago. Orthodox Jewish men are not supposed to physically touch women other than their wife or children. Well, a pregnant woman was on this bus. And this Orthodox man wouldn't let her sit down because he feared she would get too close to him. Most people on the bus saw this transpiring but did nothing. My mom went up to this Hasidic Jew and, in fluent Hebrew, told him, "You're going to hell and even though you dress like a religious man, you're not holy at all." Telling a religious Jew they won't be accepted into "the world to come" is about as heavy an insult that could be levied. My mom cut through him so effortlessly. She verbally obliterated him and gave zero fucks because she always stood for what was right. She never cared about how she would be perceived if she was on the right side of what was good.

"Seriously, what about my kids?"

My mom doubled down.

"Ileana spends much more time with the kids than you. And because of all that time she puts in, and the time you put in too, when you're not thinking about yourself or irrelevant people like Don Lemon or Tucker Carlson, they're smart. I'm sure it's from genetics too. They analyze things and understand so much about the world around them. Even Judah who is still only four. They have a sense of humor. They have personality; they have opinions. What is there not to like about them?"

"How does it happen that they form these distinct person-alities so young?"

"I told you: I think it's underlying genetics combined with parenting and also the position they are in the family. Middle children are usually different than first born. You're the baby, and you still act like one!"

I ignored her. And asked a question I knew would make her nervous, especially since this was all being documented for the world to read, or at least our family and friends.

"You clearly favored me and seem to love me a little more than your daughter. Why?"

"You're sick. I mean you have problems. On my life, it's not true."

I mouthed, "You can tell me."

She smiled. I laughed. Whenever my mom used the expression, "On my life," you knew she was in a defensive stance, working to proclaim her innocence.

"On my life. I swear to you, it's not true."

My mom had always described our relationship as symbiotic. It was a little more twisted than that if we are both being honest. I mean who else would write a book like this?

"So, let me rephrase my question," I interjected. "Do parents, like yourself, for example, have a tendency to maybe not love, but favor, one child over another?"

"The word is not favor. It's possible, though, there is more of a genetic overlap with one of the children than with the other one."

I was beginning to break her into submission. I have amazing endurance when it comes to being annoying.

"Do you think it's common for one parent to gravitate toward one of their kids more than another?"

"I don't gravitate towards you. I'm just a sucker for what you have to offer. Arden offers a whole other set of lovable qualities. Let me tell you what you don't offer."

In my mind, she admitted she favors me. I won this war. Arden, if you're reading, know that Dad favors you a hair more, and I'm okay with it. My mom wasn't okay with how she was just manipulated in her eyes. She saw that iPhone recording our conversation.

"Your sister is reliable; you can count on her. She knows how to organize and takes care of business. She's willing to do unpleasant things because she feels she should. All these things she does, you don't do."

"What do I do?"

"You are like the cricket and your sister, the ant. You entertain; you are fun and funny. You are basically a bullshitter like me. You are charming."

"What's the cricket and the ant have to do with this?" My mom would often drop Hungarian or Serbian allegories, and I usually had no idea what she was talking about.

"What do I have to do with the cricket and the ant?"

"You don't know that story?" A playbook Jewish mom move, answering a question with a question. My mom excels at this. "The cricket spends the whole summer playing the violin. It plays music. It entertains. It enjoys itself."

"Yeah?"

"And the ant works! The ant puts its nose to the grindstone and makes sure the queen ant is taken care of. Your sister is the ant. You're the cricket."

Whatever.

"Children, like life, are meant to be enjoyed. That's the key. You should get a kick out of your kids and be excited to see them and spend time with them."

Speaking of enjoying one's children, I found a dark, depressing segue to dampen my mom's now jovial mood. Maybe my issues are more serious than anyone gives me credit?

"Your own stepfather admitted to you that he was destroyed after his only son was gassed in Auschwitz. He wanted to have your half sister as payback to the Nazis. You told me that's why you wanted to have four sons. You had your first son, Rami, and he died. How did that affect you?"

"I was happy. It felt great," my mom answered sarcastically. "Are you trying to kill me?"

I really wasn't. Perhaps the only thing I knew less about as a child than my mom's Holocaust story was the one about my brother. I don't even think I knew his name until I was in college and finally mustered up the courage to ask. I had never visited his gravesite. In fact, I didn't even know where he was buried. My parents had never visited him.

"This is painful. I felt very badly when I found out he was sick. There's really no way to describe what this did to me. When we got the diagnosis, I was so heartbroken I had to leave. It was my only viable response. So, I left the baby with your Grandma Helen. She was a masochist, may Helen rest in peace, and she loved taking care of a sick baby. Me and your father went to Europe. We went to Venice and took Arden with us. If I had stayed, I would've died."

I couldn't help but notice the similarities with the loss of her son and the loss of her family in the Holocaust. In each, she had to escape for her own survival. It wasn't just a coping mechanism. It was a necessary tool for survival. Who could judge? Surely no one who had never walked in her shoes.

In this book's chapter on marriage, my mother openly admitted that leaving Israel stressed her relationship more than the death of a child. I tried to wrap my head around this, even trying to imagine myself in her place, God forbid, but I still couldn't understand how this could be possible. I asked her about this again.

"I don't owe you or anyone, for that matter, an explanation. These things are very personal."

I looked down at that same screen saver of my three children and realized I could never get past it if something happened to one of them. How did my mom have such strength? How did she move on?

"I remember calling my stepfather and telling him—I remember this, more or less, word for word, for some reason—I said, 'We are young, we are going to find a solution. And we will be fine.'"

My mom, now an overprotective grandmother and great-grandmother, promised me not to discuss the specific disease that killed my older brother. Not because she was embarrassed or wanted to hide, but because she's slightly paranoid and very practical and did not want to prejudice any potential suitors for her own grandchildren. The journalist in me begrudgingly agreed to her terms for this very exclusive interview.

"On that magical day when you found out you were pregnant with me, were you excited or nervous, or both?"

I'm fifty-four, and I had never asked that question before. We had hardly ever even discussed any of this.

"I wasn't excited at all. And I was extremely nervous."

"Well, this explains a lot. You weren't excited about me."

"This isn't about you, Joel."

Here we go again.

"Dr. Gold was the name of the pediatric neurologist in Manhattan. He was the best in the field."

One genetic trait the Jewish people writ large inherited is always following a doctor's name by the phrase "the best." It's the Eleventh Commandment.

"How do you know he was the best?"

My mom laughed. "In this case, he really was. He was the world expert in this disease. He confirmed our son Rami was afflicted with it, and he told us we had his sympathy. I didn't want anyone's sympathy. But he told us almost too honestly that this baby will be a big problem for us."

I was born on July 25, 1969 in St. Peter's Hospital in New Brunswick, New Jersey. Incidentally, another Jew who would rise to a little more prominence than me, actor Michael

Douglas, was born in this same Catholic hospital twenty-five years earlier almost to the day.

"Rami was born July 23rd, 1967, two years before you."

When you write a book, you find out unbelievable things that you should've probably already known, like your only brother's birthday. I had never known his birthday until now. Why did I know so little? I guess the short answer is my mother wanted to protect me from all the pain she experienced when I was much too young to fully understand any of it. My brother and I are both Leos. *Wow*, I thought.

"Rami was in St. Peter's Hospital dying as you were born."

"Do you remember which floors we were on?"

"All I remember is Rami was above you. And you were both surrounded by crucifixes, which gave me some comfort because it reminded me of Matilda Goricanec, the nun who saved me."

Maybe I should have left this part out of the book, I thought. I knew it was flooding my mom with horrific memories as she was dealing with my father now in a nursing home himself. At least he was in Miami Jewish and not Miami Catholic, I thought, stealing a page from my mom's optimism playbook.

"Rami's condition regressed so much there was nothing else the doctors or the nurses at St. Peter's could do for him. He was like how your dad is now, getting worse and worse."

I could tell my mom was much more upset about my father's current condition. But she continued to tell me about the brother who I never really knew and was just now learning so much about.

"He had to be tube fed, and he was in very bad shape. He wasn't developing. He couldn't stand or walk or even sit by himself without flopping over."

"What was it like for you to watch that?"

"I watched it as little as humanly possible. But whenever I did see him, it was so very, very sad."

"When did he finally get sent to that home in Pennsylvania?"

"I have no idea when he was sent there. I'd say six months after you were born. I focus on the negative as little as possible. But I still remember the name. It was called the Lynch House. It was for very sick children, full of vegetables."

I was going to tell my mom that "vegetable" was no longer a politically correct term. But even I didn't think this was an appropriate time to weigh in on something I know she couldn't give a shit about.

"How old was he when he died?"

"He was three or four. I don't know exactly when he died."

I was stunned and fascinated at once. In the oddest way possible, this epitomized my mom, I realized. She had to push the pain from her memory to survive. It's not that she didn't want to remember when her eldest son died. It's that she could not if she wanted to move on.

I wondered for a moment what others reading this might think. Instantly I heard my mother's voice in my head, even though she was sitting two feet from me, saying, "Fuck everyone." Pleasing others was never her modus operandi. Doing what was right for her and her family was all that ever mattered. My mom often invoked another Hungarian saying, "The dogs bark and the caravan passes." No matter what people would say or think, she wanted us to continue to move forward steadily like that caravan.

"Do you know if you ever took me to visit him?"

"No. For what?"

She was unrepentant.

"He was a vegetable. I never even let you play with him because he couldn't play. He was too sick."

"Why not at least let us be together?" I asked.

"I decided I'm not going to make this tragedy the center of my life or yours. It was a difficult but conscious decision.

"He died by the time you were two years old."

My mom had this look on her face that I recognized. It came about when she felt pushed a bit too far. And now was one of those times.

"Joel, let me tell you something. There was an organization for parents whose children suffered from the same disease as Rami. Most parents jerked off to this."

My mom loves to be crude for emphasis. She'll be mortified reading this and will beg me to delete it. But I never would, and she will ultimately appreciate that I allowed you to see how she really thinks and speaks.

"You have no idea what it was like. People had birthday parties for these babies and took pictures and had all sorts of memorial ceremonies. Many couples we knew in this world divorced from the stress of it all. Parents drowned themselves in the drama; some almost reveled in it. Your father and I decided we wouldn't participate in any of it. That was not my life; that was not the way it was going to be. Period."

"Were you and Dad in denial about this child?"

"No. It was real. Too real. It one hundred percent all happened. It's not a form of denial. Again, it all one hundred percent happened. Other parents made this the central tragedy of their lives. This was their life script, their big drama."

"But how could you separate yourself from your very own child?"

During my reporting years, I wrote countless stories on parents who lost children to illness or accidents or mass shootings. I had never met another parent like my own mother who was able to separate herself from her ill or fallen child so seamlessly. I wondered: Was there something seriously wrong with my mom? I convinced myself there wasn't. She experienced different things in her life and handled a very personal tragedy in an equally personal way. Then she said something that caught me off guard.

"Our situation was different. You must understand that our baby, at just six months old, already had a death sentence. He was incapable of developing. They regress, move backwards in age in their abilities. Our baby couldn't sit. He couldn't turn. He couldn't turn on his own for Christ's sake."

My mom was convincing herself that her child was worse off than one with cancer. And, while we both knew this wasn't true, who was I to question how she reacted to it all?

"I remember even thinking I don't want your dad's sperm to impregnate me again because I couldn't go through it again."

I squirmed, ironically just like sperm, at my mother's use of this very visual and visceral word.

"But I couldn't hide. Your father and I did it, and we eventually conceived you."

After I got past "we did it," I realized my mom reemerged stronger after the Holocaust and losing her firstborn son. This was an amazing lesson in courage and resilience. And one that could only ever be taught through actions and not words.

"Is it true that I was one of the first children in America tested for this disease?" I had vaguely remembered my mom once telling me this.

"It's one hundred percent the truth. You were tested at the National Institutes of Health near Washington, DC. But because the testing and research was so new, we wouldn't get the results for eight months. I thought I would die having to wait that long. And you were going to be a full-term baby, and you were coming out of my vagina no matter what."

"Could you please not say that?"

"Vagina, vagina, vagina," my mom tripled down.

"How stressed out were you?"

"More stressed out than either Don Lemon or Tucker Carlson is right now."

"That's too bad. I wish their level of stress was infinitely worse," I snapped back so quickly it almost made my mom proud, if it weren't so stupid in her eyes.

"When you were eight months, someone at the NIH called and told us you appeared to be healthy, but because the research was so new there was a caveat that the testing could be wrong."

"So, after I was born, were you distant with me?"

"Yes."

It's incredible that I never knew any of this until now. *It is amazing*, I thought, *how you can know so little about those you love and who love you the most.*

"Psychologically in my head, I kept you at a distance. I couldn't be sure you would be okay for five or six months after you were born. One of the symptoms is cherry red spots inside the eye. If you didn't have those, we knew you'd be okay."

"I'm still not okay mentally," I joked. My mom laughed too.

"I meant that you would be safe from this genetic disease. I never said anything about your current, stunted mental state."

"So eventually you went to the doctor again in Manhattan to get my eyes checked?"

"Well, not exactly!"

She cracked a wry smile.

"The night before our long-scheduled appointment, I mysteriously developed a one hundred three–degree fever, and I couldn't move. I was feeling sick. We had a nanny who went with your father. I stayed in bed. There were no cell phones then. No text messages. I was sick to my stomach waiting for that damn phone to ring. And finally, it did."

"And Dad told you perfection was delivered!" I exclaimed with an arrogant smile.

"Believe it or not, your father was getting the car because he was too worried about getting a parking ticket. It was our nanny, and she told me about the news in French. She was Haitian, and that's how we communicated."

I couldn't get past my dad. His quirks could fill a separate book, which I hope to write someday soon, called *Surviving the Psychiatrist*. It didn't surprise me that he was more worried about paying for a parking ticket than calling my mom to tell her the great news about yours truly.

"The instant I received word you'd be a healthy child, my fever disappeared. I felt so relieved I cried. And it never felt so good."

When I was expecting my first child, a fellow newsroom friend told me you'll never experience such high highs and such low lows with anyone or anything other than your own children. And my mom's experience with her two sons is a strong testament to this very true statement.

"This all began with my thoughts on children in general. What would I have right now if I didn't have you or Arden or my eight grandchildren? And one great-grandchild? Nothing is the answer. Family is everything. I don't regret anything. Would

I have liked to have more children? Yes. But my cup overflows with life, with my children, grandchildren, and great-grandchild. I wish everyone had children so everyone could experience this level of joy!"

"One final thing about children. Am I your favorite child?"

"No. No you are not."

"You can tell me quietly. I won't publish it."

My mom looked down at my phone. She looked up at me and grinned.

"Fuck off, Joel."

I reminded her that I was *still* recording.

"You're not my favorite. I wouldn't lie to you. I can rely more on Arden. But you're okay too."

Actual Voicemail from My Mom: July 25, 2022

Jo-el,

Remember what my mother said: "If it's a money problem, it's not really a problem."

Do not stress out. Roy and I will help you. You see your father worried about money his whole life, and now he can't walk and has accidents at night.

You're worrying about the wrong thing.

Okay.

Love you.

It's your hostess with the most-ess, your mother.

"IF IT'S A MONEY PROBLEM, IT'S NOT A PROBLEM"

In the early days of *Surviving the Survivor*, before we were a true crime podcast, we'd interview all sorts of interesting, high-profile thought leaders.

One of these people was Dr. Avi Loeb. He's an astrophysicist at Harvard University who believes he saw an alien spacecraft deep in the universe. I had fallen into a bad habit of asking some of these notable guests to mention us to their minions so we could build our show. My mom hated that I was doing this. She is never one to ask anyone for help. I'd describe her as a giver, not a taker, while I may fall into the latter category. So, while we were on air, as I was about to ask Dr. Loeb to help us spread the *Surviving the Survivor* gospel, my mom interrupted.

"Joel, what did I tell you?"

"Dr. Loeb, my mom has instituted a new rule on our show. I must now ask each of our guests how I can help them."

Dr. Loeb, a brilliant, fun, gregarious intellectual, laughed at the exchange unfolding before him.

"Always listen to your mother," Dr. Loeb jokingly admonished me as he spoke with a hint of an Israeli accent.

"Don't dare embarrass me, and do not ask the professor for anything, Joel."

We'd argue back and forth as our guests, most of whom had been on countless other shows, watched with enjoyment, curiosity, and a bit of bewilderment. They weren't used to being on any platform with an argumentative mother and son.

"Fine," I relented. "Dr. Loeb is there anything we can do for you?"

Without missing a beat, Dr. Loeb responded with a wry smile, "Can you help me get one hundred fifty million dollars for a new telescope?"

I wasn't sure if he was serious. I looked at him. I looked at my mom. He was indeed serious. At the time of our interview, the professor was making headlines around the world for observing what he believed was an extraterrestrial spacecraft in a distant galaxy. He was on every news show imaginable, in every newspaper. He was ubiquitous. He even told us a movie was being made about him and his discovery, and he was hoping Brad Pitt would play him.

"You need one hundred fifty million dollars?" I repeated, trying to hide the incredulity in my voice.

"Roughly, yes. Give or take a few million," he responded. He wasn't joking.

I think he believed I could help him raise this money.

"Please don't institute any new rules on this show anymore," I told my mom.

We all laughed. But his request hit me like a meteor for a completely different reason.

He's among the best-known astrophysicists in the world, and he needed one thing: money.

Money recently became my singular obsession. My OCD brain has a tendency to latch on to things like a K9 on to its suspect. I just couldn't let it go.

Until I was around fifty, I admittedly never thought much about money. I grew up comfortably, and the emphasis in my home and among my circle of friends was always heavily weighted on education. Most of my adult life, I was more preoccupied with rising in my career trajectory and getting a position as a national news correspondent. Unless you're one of the top personalities in news, salaries are notoriously low. It's about stature, not making money, and I just never cared about the financial side of things.

My dad, a product of the Great Depression, would always tell me, "Joel, fools chase respect. Smart people chase money." I never listened.

I now had my own company, my own podcast, and most importantly, my own family, but I was missing the financial security that comes with being part of a traditional media company. There were no more steady paychecks and health insurance coverage. Everyone was depending on me, and the pressure was really beginning to build.

How come I never got the money memo? I wondered. In the American education system, we're never taught about financial literacy, and that's a serious problem, since money is crucial to living well.

To make matters worse, I was now living in Miami Beach, where the only thing more plentiful than beaches, Botox, and babes is money. The city is dripping in it.

Dr. Loeb's request was weighing on me on our ride home. I wish I could've helped him. More importantly, at fifty-four, I yearned to be more independent. If I had more money, I'd never need to ask my parents for help again. I wanted to be the giver now, not the taker.

"When you hear the word 'money,' what is your first association?" I asked my mom sitting beside me in the car. I knew I was opening Pandora's box.

"I am totally neutral. I don't have any emotional attachment to money. Unlike you, I don't get anxious about it. I don't get overjoyed about it. I'm just very neutral about it," she explained.

The only thing that made me more anxious than money itself was being lectured by my mom about it, which I knew was about to happen. I could feel myself gripping the steering wheel so hard my knuckles were white.

One of my dad's favorite stories was about the famous bank robber Willie Sutton. After finally being caught, newspaper reporters asked him why he robbed banks, and he matter-of-factly answered, "That's where the money is."

My dad chuckled every time he told me this. He and Willie Sutton were both practical. Money doesn't solve all problems, but it helps with many. My dad grasped this from a young age seeing poverty-stricken people selling apples on the Grand Concourse in the Bronx. Willie Sutton certainly understood this, and that's why he robbed banks. But I never really got it. Until now. And it seemed too late.

We were stopped at a traffic light, and my mom's focus wandered. She was looking at a heavily tattooed, pierced couple walking hand in hand.

"Joel, don't dare get a tattoo. You don't have any, do you?"

"Please focus, Mom. How do you explain Dad's Willie Sutton story?" I asked, because we had all heard it a thousand times.

"I am focused. You're not focused."

She took her eyes off the punk-rock-looking couple to glare at me. She continued, "I understand the Willie Sutton story—that if you need something, you should know where to go to get it. If you need love, you look at a different place than if you need money. When you need money, you go to the bank."

"I'm beginning to think it's one of life's most important resources. Willie knew stealing was illegal, and it's not something a person of sound mind would ever do, but desperate times called for desperate measures. Willie Sutton robbed banks because money is *that* important."

"I see him as a crook," my mom responded flatly.

"You always tell me that Grandma Anyu, may she rest in peace for all eternity, would say, wait, what would she say? I forget, exactly."

"First of all, it needs to be told in context, otherwise it sounds weird. But she always said, 'If it is a money problem, it's not a problem.'"

"By the way, do you think Grandma Anyu is dancing and smiling in the world to come?"

"No, I don't. Do you want to discuss money or stupidity?"

"Grandma Anyu had no money."

"Do you know she grew up so poor that her father couldn't afford an apartment with regular floors? They lived in these cheap apartments where the floor was literally made of dirt."

It was all so crazy. In a matter of just three generations, my grandmother went from dirt floors to her grandson living in Miami Beach with a pool and jacuzzi. She apparently never worried about money, but now, it's all I ever thought about. *How could life be so absurd?* I thought again, as we continued our drive.

"What did Grandma Anyu's father do?" I asked, having no clue. I was reminded once again how little I knew about my own flesh and blood.

"Your great-grandfather taught in a religious school. But they were refugees living in a new land with almost no means to just get by."

One of the running jokes that irritated my mom beyond measure was when I'd ask her if her friends that I had met at her condo had children or grandchildren. The implication was that if they didn't, I'd swoop in and help them in exchange for their inheritance. She hated this. Maybe I'm shallow, what can I say? I was entering dangerous territory with my mom.

"When Grandma Anyu left this lovely planet, how much money did she leave you?"

"It amazes me how stupid you are. Is this any of your business?" But my mom answered anyway, "This is how beautiful it was. She didn't owe anybody money, and she didn't leave a penny to anybody either."

"She literally left you nothing?"

"Zero."

I got so anxious in that moment thinking what would happen to me if I got nothing. I'd certainly end up in a soup kitchen with my wife and kids. Why did I not care more about money earlier in life? What was wrong with me?

"Well, she left me a gold bracelet that she bought herself after the war. But that's it."

I stared at the few pieces of jewelry on my mom's hand and realized I wouldn't get by too long with just that. My stomach was turning along with my steering wheel.

"And when Grandma Helen passed?"

"That's an interesting story." My mom's focus strayed to a stray dog, of all things. It was crossing the street, taking a far greater risk than Willie Sutton robbing banks.

"Don't look at dogs! Look at me."

"Don't tell me where to look, prick."

"I'm recording all this."

"I don't care. I will still deny it, and I'm a little old lady so who do you think they'll believe?"

We glared at each other again. It was a game of chicken to see who would crack a smile first. My mom got us back on track, which we would soon veer off of again.

"When Grandma Helen was getting older, she was very worried she'd outlive her money. She was pathologically worried, sort of like you."

"Did she leave you and Dad anything?"

"She left us her apartment and about fifty thousand dollars in cash."

"Wait, she was pathologically worried about money?" I felt reassured that I wasn't the only one.

"Yes, that she would outlive her money, and she would not have anything left. But I would scream at her and ask her what she was worrying for. I kept reminding her she had three sons: two doctors and one architect. I told her they would take care of her."

This hit me hard. Even though they didn't need my help, I had this secret fantasy about taking care of my parents in their old age. A fantasy I wouldn't be able to turn into reality before their deaths. It made me sad.

"Mom, you know I always wanted to buy you a pink Rolls-Royce so you could show it off to your friends at the Blue and Green Diamonds. But it's not happening," I said sheepishly.

"Good, because I'd drive it into the Intracoastal. I honestly don't know how I raised such a stupid son. You should be embarrassed of yourself. Get me home so I don't need to listen to this shit. You have me held captive in this goddamn car too long. Maybe I should just open the door and roll out."

"Dad is famous for spending the better part of his life worrying about money. Do you think it was learned behavior from Grandma Helen?"

She didn't hear me. My mom was now looking at a billboard of a woman staring at a man wearing an Audemars Piguet watch.

"She only wants to fuck him because of his watch!" I blurted out. "Everything is about money. Money makes the world go around. You're looking at proof right there on the billboard!"

"Pull over. I can't be around you."

We were on I-195. For a brief moment, I wanted to drop my mom off on the shoulder.

"What do you attribute Dad's money worries to?" I rephrased the question for my mom.

"To his own life experience."

"Elaborate. Don't give me five-word answers for this book, otherwise—I already told you—it will be a magazine article. Give me a story for *your* book. This is *your memoir*." I snapped at her. I knew the subject of money would get us both testy.

"I'll wipe my ass with it." My mom returned to the outrageous as a warning shot to back off and then dropped an insult on top of it. "This book will never be about me. It will be all about *you*!"

Mel Brooks just published his autobiography called *All About Me*! I was so jealous he came up with that title before me.

But that's probably why he's one of the greatest comedy writers of all time and I'm not!

It was a beautiful day. The Sunshine State was living up to its name with bathers and fishermen littering the shores of Biscayne Bay. I wondered for a brief second how I lasted so many years living in such shit weather in New Jersey and New York City. I really appreciated where I was now, even though I wished I was making more dough. We got back to my dad and his lifelong money concerns.

"He lived in a crappy two-bedroom apartment in the Bronx. It was your dad, his two brothers, and parents all crammed into this place on Marion Avenue. It was very hot in the summers, and there was no air conditioning. But your Grandpa Milton still sent them to Camp Mohican in the Berkshires. It was a real luxury back then, and even though Grandpa Milton couldn't afford it, he still sent them. The building's superintendent used to bang on the door asking for the rent. And he would not have the money. He used it all on camp. The super always threatened to evict them."

If I was short on money, my parents were just a call away. My grandfather had no one to call. What if that was me? What would I do? I felt sick to my stomach. I'm so fortunate but still feel so vulnerable like everything could come crumbling down any second. I had inherited my mom's World War Two paranoia and my dad's Great Depression financial angst.

"That knocking on the door was very, very uncomfortable for your father. It was a jarring sound that stayed with your dad until now, I think. He's always been worried about getting that knock on the door asking for money. He has PTD."

"It's PTSD. It's post-traumatic stress disorder. The word 'stress' is in there for a reason."

I don't think my mom realized her paranoia evolved from something so similar: a knock on the door from the Nazis who grabbed her father and dragged him into the infamous Auschwitz gas chambers. These bizarre parallels, whether I liked them or not, were part of my fabric. It was weaved into my being, I realized.

"I don't think the poverty in the streets of New York bothered him as much as his parents constantly fighting over money. Grandma Helen wanted Grandpa Milton to work at the post office so he had a steady job. But Grandpa Milton refused. He refused to work for anyone else and had his own business cutting plastic used as inserts in wallets. He was a terrible businessman, but he only wanted to work for himself."

The other side of the family, also Holocaust survivors, eventually took over my Grandpa Milton's business and turned it into a behemoth plastics company. *Why didn't I go into plastics?* I wondered. *What the hell does plastics even mean?*

"Why did I go into television news and not plastics?" I asked my mom, making a critical mistake as I knew I would get blasted for asking this.

"Joel, you went into TV news for the same reason as the man who cleans the elephant's shit in the circus. So, when they ask him what he does he can say, 'I'm in show business!'"

My mom loved to tell me this.

"Let's face it. You're not really interested in money. You wanted something exciting, something where people would notice you," she lambasted me.

I was squeezing the steering wheel even harder. But I knew she was partly right too. A mobile billboard truck drove by us with an ad for a new sex lubricant. It featured a hot woman sucking on a moist strawberry.

"Your brain needs lubricating," my mom said without missing a beat.

"Are you focused?"

"I am totally focused. You are not focused."

"Would you say Grandpa Milton lived paycheck to paycheck?"

"No, because he wasn't getting a weekly paycheck. There were months at a time where customers wouldn't pay him, and that's why he couldn't pay his rent so often."

I grew up in such a cocoon. My dad always had money to pay the mortgage. There were never any knocks at our door. The only knocks I heard were in my head. And, with each day, they grew louder. Why had I never focused more on money? Was it all my fault?

"Do you think Dad's motivation to become a doctor was as much financial as it was to help people?"

"No, he didn't do it to help people. He loved helping people. But he became a doctor because of everything he experienced around him growing up. And he knew becoming a doctor, at a time when physicians made a good living, was his only way out of escaping those knocks on his door."

My head was pounding like those knocks on the door.

"Roy's father told him he had to go to dental school because he knew he wouldn't be a good businessman. Grandpa Milton gave him no choice. That's why your Uncle Seymour is an architect, and Uncle Ron is a doctor too. They couldn't risk being poor businessmen after what they all saw growing up."

"Why weren't any of them good businessmen?" I wanted to know.

"This may be politically incorrect but who cares. They weren't conniving enough. They weren't greedy enough. They were more intellectual."

It hit me like a ton of matzah balls. Why the hell am I even writing this book? If I was really interested in making money, maybe I should be working to start my own plastics business. Is my ego preventing me from growing my wealth? I was in the midst of a Jean-Paul Sartre–sized existential crisis during the relatively short drive from our podcast studio to my mom's condo.

"When you and Dad were married and began life together in 1961, what would you say your total net worth was at that time?" I wanted to know. I knew it was low and would make me feel a tiny bit better about myself.

"I know exactly to the penny: one thousand four hundred dollars."

"How do you know that?"

"Because we didn't have a single penny between us. At our wedding, we had twenty-four relatives. They knew we needed money, and they all gave us cash. And it totaled one thousand four hundred dollars. I keep track of my money."

My mom never missed an opportunity to drive the dagger a little further into my chest. She knew I was a little fiscally irresponsible and found a slight opening to nail home that point.

"What do you attribute your relative success to?"

Over the last sixty-plus years, my parents accumulated a fair amount of wealth. They invested wisely in real estate and other ventures.

During the editing of this book, I got a frantic call from my mom.

"Are you out of your frigging zombie mind? You're going to tell the entire world our financial history?"

"I thought you told me no one was ever going to read this book, so what does it really matter?"

She was upset I had included more details than she was comfortable with.

Needless to say I was forced, with the threat of being left out of an inheritance, into deleting some information originally included in this masterpiece.

"This will sound like a dig or that I'm preaching," my mom continued. I was almost grateful to her for warning me of the insult she was about to hurl my way.

"Unlike you, we got nothing from our parents. There was nothing to give."

Here we go, I thought. This was about to be the shock and awe of insults. Fire was incoming, and I was preparing mentally, already exhausted from our two-hour podcast and seemingly endless drive back home.

"Your father worked very, very hard. And he worked very long hours from seven a.m. until ten p.m. with only two interruptions: one for lunch and one for dinner."

"I worked hard," I said in my defense.

"Joel, be honest with yourself. From the first year we started to work, your dad said to me, 'We must save up money for our retirement.' He saved, Joel. He planned, and he saved."

The guilt was overwhelming. For a moment, I thought about telling my mom about the Tod's loafers I bought for $800 at Bal Harbour Shops, one of the most high-end malls in America, just a few blocks from my home. I had also bought a pair of sunglasses I saw on the show *White Lotus*, which I couldn't get off my mind. I told you my OCD brain latches on to things and can't let go. I was so close to confessing all this to my mom in a moment of weakness and then realized what a stupid move it would be. But the guilt was coursing through my veins. I shook my head out to bring myself back into this conversation about money.

"So, what do you attribute your success to?"

"I'm telling you, schmuck. We did what you and your wife never do. We saved. We built it up. And we never lived beyond our means."

My family and I lived in a neighborhood we had no business being in, only being able to live there because we bought just before the pandemic and before south Florida home values skyrocketed to values I could never afford now.

"We built our small wealth slowly. We saved. We didn't spend on stupidity."

I couldn't get the image of those Tod's loafers or Mykita sunglasses out of my head. I was literally trying to blink them away. I should never have bought either.

"Do you have an eyelash in your eye?"

"No!"

To make matters worse, those Mykita sunglasses are made in Germany. Since the war, my mom refused to buy anything made in Germany. How could I betray her by buying Mykita sunglasses? The war was so long ago, and these sunglasses were so cool, I tried to convince myself.

"We never lived above what we made. Do you see that?"

"Yes," I answered sheepishly.

My parents were the least ostentatious people I knew. They owned cars for decades. They wore the same clothes even longer. They rarely splurged. I felt like I was in the middle of a scene from *Saving Private Ryan* with verbal bombs exploding all around me as I had vivid flashbacks of all the stupid shit I spent ridiculous amounts of money on. My guilt level was at DEFCON 10.

"Your father never wanted new clothes. I forced him to buy a suit jacket. He refused to even try it on. He just didn't care. And I only shopped at Loehmann's. Remember Loehmann's?"

How could I forget? Loehmann's was a dump of a discount store in neighboring East Brunswick, New Jersey, where all the Jewish women hunted for good finds. I loved going there as a kid because some of these vultures would tear their clothes off right in the middle of the aisle to beat the next predator to the deal.

"When we visited Grandma Anyu, we didn't stay in fancy hotels like you and your wife. We were fine with three-star hotels. We didn't need to impress our friends with the Ritz or what's the other one?"

"The Four Seasons," I answered without thinking, just handing the heavy artillery to my mom now.

"We were always very conscious of saving. Some years, we even borrowed money from the bank—borrowed money from the bank in the end of the year to put it into our retirement plan because we had a tax-free retirement plan, an IRA where we could put money in if we had it. But we usually didn't have it. So, we borrowed money from the bank to put it in our savings. We worked on it very hard and nonstop because we knew nobody would hand us anything."

"I know you're getting a little bit older, but can you at least try to make your digs against me a touch more subtle?"

"It's one hundred percent a dig against you and your wife. And I don't care because you need to hear the truth. You two live very differently from us. You say things like, 'I deserve it,' or 'I'm going to treat myself to it.' You don't deserve shit. Work and save, and don't be indulgent. And you and your wife can call me a bitch. Ask me if I care?"

"I'd never call my sweet, soothing, elderly mother such a name," I said, clutching the steering wheel as though it was the only thing keeping me tethered to earth.

My mom was now, understandably, distracted by a man wearing a feathered boa walking mini–Italian greyhounds in matching denim outfits. Miami is a wild place.

"Pay attention to me, not the queer guy with the eye for the greyhound guy."

"How the hell am I supposed to ignore this?" My mom tried not to laugh. "I am collecting my thoughts. I'm not wandering away. I can look at him and those beautiful dogs and still tell you what I'm thinking. I can multitask."

"What would Dad privately say to you about money?"

"Karmela, we have to save. We have to save. We have to save. We have to save. It was his mantra. Yours is spend, spend, spend! He wasn't stingy and let me buy whatever I wanted. But I never wanted much."

My mom stuck her tongue out at me. She was loving being able to rub all this in.

"Okay, so besides the Willie Sutton story, Dad also famously used to tell me not to ever marry a church mouse like he did with you. What did he mean by that?"

"Well, church mice are in trouble because there is no food in churches. So, there's no cheese to be had."

As if this conversation wasn't stress-inducing enough, my mom was taking forever to get through a sentence. "Speed it up. This is a conversation, not a thought bubble.

"I am speaking slowly. I'm walking slowly. I'm thinking slowly, and I'm legally entitled to all of this at my age, okay?"

"So, the church mouse?"

"Like I just explained, we had not a penny. Roy said he made two mistakes. One of which is that he married a very poor girl, me. Second, he claimed he never had a life plan. Other doctors were making a lot of money owning clinics and being entrepreneurial. He always thought he could've been making more money. I had no life plan other than to survive in a rough world, and I've been very happy just being okay."

"Your son, me, had everything, unlike his parents, given to him. And I feel like I am living paycheck to paycheck. I am constantly in a state of stress, feeling like I'm going to have an aneurysm any minute over money. Why?"

"It's because you're dumb!"

"Dumb? That's it? All you have to say is I'm dumb?"

"I think, in general, you are expecting others, like me or someone else in this world, to take care of you. You have balls, don't you? Grab them once in a while."

"I am literally sick to my stomach, to the point where I cannot open my Bank of America app because it stresses me out so much."

"I can't cure stupidity."

"Do you have anything else to say?"

"Yes, you are a coward. Cowards die a thousand deaths. You are afraid to look at your bank account? I wanted strong, brave sons. I guess I'll have to wait until my next life, which is just around the corner."

"Why can't I accumulate wealth like you and Dad?"

"Because the two of you are not the type to save. You're both spoiled brats. And I don't care if Ileana gets mad at me. I'll tell her right to her face. You're both master manipulators. And, for whatever reason, we give in and help you with what you need. We're idiots too."

"Are you worried about my financial security?"

"Not everything is about you, Joel. No, I'm not. I have bigger worries. Your father is basically a vegetable right now."

"I can't do these kids birthday parties or school events anymore because every time I attend anything, I'm reminded of how badly I failed in the money-making department. Earlier today, I found out Jacob's dad makes thirty-five million dollars a year with his hedge fund. How do I reconcile that? How do I not feel like a complete loser?"

"Who said you're not a complete loser? You're a loser and a stupid one at that. And, if we're being honest, you're less achieving than Jacob's dad. Your penis is probably smaller too."

I was shocked that I hadn't snapped the steering wheel from the dashboard with the amount of force this stress was creating.

"He has his talent. And you have yours."

"Objectively, besides family and health, what's more important than money in this world? If you have money, it eliminates almost all your stress."

"That's what you think, moron. It's amazing that I raised someone so dumb."

"Convince me otherwise."

"You don't think visiting your father in the nursing home is stressful?"

"I said besides family and health, nothing is more important than money. And even that's debatable."

"I hope God doesn't punish you for your stupidity."

"I'm trying to teach my kids now that there are two types of people in the world: people who shop at Target and people who create Target. I never got that kind of fiscal lesson from you, not ever."

"Your father and I aren't as dumb as you. We wanted to make sure you had a good education and a career, which you did and still do. You created *Surviving the Survivor* from nothing, and now you have over one hundred thousand subscribers and one million views a month."

Did she just slip a compliment in?

"Yes, but I'm not making thirty-five million a year like Jacob's dad. I don't give a shit about my kids getting an education. I want them on the sidewalk selling lemonade and learning about business and money."

"I feel sorry for your kids."

"Well, maybe they won't worry about opening their Bank of America app."

"By then, I'm sure it'll be implanted in their brain, and there won't even be apps."

"And I hope my kids invent those neural brain implants."

"Elon Musk is already doing it."

"That's another thing! All the good ideas are already taken."

"Get me home now. I'm afraid this stupidity could be contagious."

We finally turned onto Collins Avenue, a famous Miami Beach street, lined with condos on one side and multimillion dollar mansions on the other side of the Intracoastal.

"What do you think when you look at all these mansions?" I pointed over to them.

"So, help me God, I feel sorry for them. First, they're not on the beach. Second, imagine having to clean them? It must be so lonely in such a big house."

"They're not worrying about paying bills. They're not calculating numbers in their head after they buy Reese's Peanut

Butter Cups at CVS to make sure there is enough money in their bank account!"

"I am very sorry, Joel. I do not want to talk to you any longer because what you are saying to me is so stupid and absurd. I know you're trying to get a rise out of me."

Maybe I was a little guilty of this too. But the subject of money really does stress me out beyond measure. My mom took a deep breath.

"I am very aware of money. I am totally conscious of money. I am not a Pollyanna, but it's just not that important to me. I have self-value without money."

"How?"

"Come into the condominium where I live. It's filled with very rich people. And you know what? They're all dying too. They show off their Teslas and, and, what's the other one?"

"Rolls-Royce? Bentley?"

"Yes, and I swear to you, their lives are even more meaningless. Imagine putting value and self-worth into a car? They are stupid like you. Uncle Alan, may he rest in peace, for all his money, was very uneducated and unsophisticated."

Right on cue, we pulled into the parking area. In front of us was a light pink Rolls-Royce straight out of Miami Beach central casting.

"That color is perfect for you, Joel."

"I swear to God I'll key that fucking car."

"I think life has so much more to offer than money. Money is useful for paying rent or whatever you absolutely need it for."

"Now, let me ask you something else, Mom."

"No, please don't. You have an incurable disease. You may die from this disease."

"What's the disease?"

"It's envy and greed."

"Jacob's dad just ordered a custom Porsche 911 Sport Classic, which I know zero about, but I do know it starts at like two hundred seventy thousand dollars. I can barely afford a dozen eggs without worrying about my monthly bills. How do you think that makes me feel as a man?"

"I know. You feel like somebody cut off your penis. It's because you have no self-worth. Maybe Ileana is cheating on you because you don't have enough money?"

My mom took such pleasure in piling more angst on top of my other angst.

"I wouldn't blame her," I said.

Karm turned to me and took on a more serious tone.

"To me, money is a joke because beyond a certain level, it's pointless how much you have. You can't sit on two chairs at once. You can only sit on one chair. You can only really enjoy one thing at a time."

"I could find comfort on two chairs. I would just slide them together."

"What don't you have in life right now? Name one thing you don't have!"

"It's not that I don't have…"

"I want to hear the answer to my question. Answer my question!"

"I don't have a private jet." I cracked a smile.

"It's not funny. You are so stupid. You were stupid as a child too." She had to attack my innocence too.

"I don't have the ability to just go out and buy something without calculating math in my head. And, this month, for example, I'm already worried about the bills. And I need to rely on Mommy and Daddy at fifty-four."

"You don't rely on Mommy and Daddy. Don't even say that because now you are making your own money."

"It ain't thirty-five million a year!"

This was all so exhausting.

"Your problem is that you never worry when you are buying things. You only worry at the end of the month when you pay bills."

I was thinking I should probably return at least one pair of those Tod's loafers. But how could I let go of them? They were so nice looking. And the leather is like a baby's ass it's so soft.

"You're allowing money to define whether you're worthy or not. It's an obsession lacking any legitimate concern. What do you not have that you would want?" my mom asked again.

"I want the ability to take my children to India next year, but I'd need Mommy's and Daddy's help for that.

"You want food poisoning?"

"Not being able to travel to India without your help makes me feel like less of a man, and it eats away at me like hydrochloric acid on a battery. I'm sure I have an ulcer."

"You know what, Joel? Very honestly, I see how exactly you live your life. You are a self-indulgent loser."

"You always say I run bad tapes in my head. What am I supposed to think? What am I supposed to say to myself to quell all the anxiety?"

"Be obsessed with whatever you want. It's your luxury. It's your right. But I'm not participating in this conversation anymore because, quite frankly, it bores me to death. And I'm close enough to death as it is right now."

My mom was halfway out of the car.

"We made a huge, huge, huge mistake, and I'm part of it. I cannot blame you that we spoiled you rotten. You're incurable."

She was almost out. I knew this next comment would get her speed up a notch. She moved like a sloth these days.

"Does Jeff Bezos wake up and worry about anything? The guy is literally worth more than the GDP of Bangladesh and about seventy other countries."

"I feel so sorry for you. You're sick. I think you're really sick. You want to be Jeff Bezos?"

"What can't he do? He can spit Jacob's dad out of his ass for fun."

"I will say this to you, Joel, no offense. I will say this to you."

Any time my mom prefaced a sentence with the phrase "no offense," which was fairly often, you knew she was about to offend you in the harshest way possible.

"I see you and I see me, and I see everybody on this planet, one hundred years from now. What do you think we will all look like? We will all be long dead in our rotting coffins underground. No amount of money will help you escape that certain destiny."

"What's the difference in your mind between five million or five hundred million?" I carried on.

"It's a number in the bank, moron. I know people who had five million and fifty million, and in the end, it was all pointless."

She was finally out of the car, scowling at me through the open passenger window.

"You know what, Joel? You are an envious person, and you are a greedy person, and you are not a very smart person because a smart person finds his own happiness. Don't tell me that happiness is only having money."

"My final question should've been my first one. Does money buy happiness?"

"Yes, but only if rich people could buy poor ones to die for them."

She looked up at the sky like she was pleading with God for help.

"I think happiness is this. It's a perfect day. It's a perfect day in Miami. It's not too windy. It's dry and not too hot. The sun is shining bright. The palm trees are swaying gently. The ocean is blue. We had a wonderful podcast. You annoyed the shit out of me on the drive home. That's happiness. That's true happiness. Our lives are made up of little chunks of happiness. And that is life."

Actual Voicemail from My Mom: July 24, 2022

Great job, Jo-el,

I just finished watching the podcast.

Excellent long day, and I'd like to know what happened behind the scenes.

To make the short story long, I love you, and I'm going to sleep. And I hope you are going to go to sleep soon also.

Bye, tweet.

"FRIENDSHIP REALLY ENRICHES LIFE"

During my Edward R. Murrow–esque media career, I had a lot of interesting jobs. Perhaps none was more eye-opening and challenging than producing "This Week in Nude News" for a live variety show, which aired in the United Kingdom in 1999, called *Michael Moore Live*. Yes, that Michael Moore: the portly guy who always wears a Michigan State hat. He thought it would be a good idea to reenact the summer's big news events—naked. It was the same summer Stephen King was badly injured in a car wreck. Do you know how hard it is to find a Stephen King look-alike who is willing to strip down to his birthday suit on live television? That was my job, and I got it done with pride. I also happened to whip everyone's ass in the *Michael Moore Live* Ping-Pong tournament. I beat Sarah Silverman's then-boyfriend in the finals as she hurled curses at me. I won a giant-ass trophy, which Michael Moore made me return. Can you believe that? But not all was lost because Michael, who had heard about my mom's Holocaust story and was intrigued, strongly encouraged me to travel to Israel and Europe to document it all. As soon as the show wrapped, I traveled to Europe and Israel to interview my mom, Grandma Anyu, other relatives, and close friends. I discovered my mom shared an unbreakable bond with a few of her friends, who had even more unbelievable stories of survival.

"They had a parcel of land in this cemetery that belonged to the family helping us. And they dug a very big grave and put a very big coffin in the ground. It was big enough for my mother and me, and that's where we hid," Rita Dunsky recounted to me while sitting in her art studio in Tel Aviv. She went on to become one of Israel's most prominent architects.

Rita, whom you'll hear more about later in this chapter, is my mom's closest friend. They met each other while both were studying at the University of Geneva. My mom had told me that Rita's story was absolutely crazy compared to hers, and it sort of was, if we're all being honest. She was hidden in a coffin with her mom.

"We stayed there during the night for like two or three months. The man helping us, who obviously wasn't Jewish and was risking his life, would bring us bread and water at night," Rita recounted.

I had trouble understanding how my mom managed to make it out alive, but this was next level. Rita was only three and a half when she experienced all this, and I just didn't understand how it was possible. The most insane part was that she had fond memories of this awful experience.

"It was a very special time for me because I was there with just my mom, and I had all of her attention, and that's where she taught me to read."

What? This reaction was incomprehensible to me. I just could not process any part of what I was hearing.

"For me, it was so nice because I was only three and half years old, but I never had to bother anyone ever again to read stories. I remember it all as a very nice memory."

Rita's story was so outrageous, it was hard to believe it was true. It made me realize the importance of my mom's friendship with Rita. Although they rarely discussed their literal war stories, their shared experience could only truly be understood by them. They knew what each had been through and how horrible it was. But, even before Rita, my mom had always valued long-lasting friendships.

"Who is the friend in this world you've known the longest?" I had never asked my mom this question until now, and I had no idea of the answer.

"Her name is Aniko Botka."

I had never heard this name before.

"How old were you when you first met her?"

"I was born August 7th, 1939. Aniko was born August 31st, 1939. I'm three weeks older than her. She lived down the street from me in Subotica in a house with three apartments inside. We knew each other before we could open our eyes; we were baby playmates. I still have a scar on my stomach from where she bit me when we were both just getting our baby teeth."

"How come I'm almost fifty-four and I've never heard her name?"

"No offense, Joel."

An offensive insult was on its way.

"Joel, I love you most in the world, but you're just not that interested usually if it's not about Joel."

"So, why am I interviewing you right now?" I countered defiantly.

"I have a funny feeling this book will be more about Joel than Karmela," she snapped back.

She might be right about this too. But whatever. My mom continued telling me about her friend Aniko.

"She was not Jewish. She is Catholic from a very aristocratic Hungarian family. Her father was a pharmacist. They owned a lot of agricultural land."

"Everyone owns real estate," I whined as this triggered my financial angst. "Even Aniko and her family in Subotica got the 'money memo.'"

"It wasn't real estate; it was land. Lots of land."

Same difference in my mind.

"I remember reuniting with Aniko after hiding in Budapest. I was very skinny, and her family invited me to one of their properties so I could rest and put some weight back on. I just remember that I only wanted to go back home to be with my mom."

"Are you still friends with her?"

"Not only are we still friends but her husband just published a book in Serbian, which I'm reading right now. It's very interesting."

My mom was always a voracious reader and still asks me how I expect to get smart if I don't read. I tell her I read plenty on X, formerly Twitter, and Instagram.

"I still don't understand how I've never heard of this woman."

"Let's move on because I don't want to insult you more."

"Why? You're going to tell me I'm selfish and self-centered? Is that what you're going to say?"

"No, I would say that you kind of glaze over things. Especially when I'm telling you stories about myself."

"I know about Rita and Bruria Werber, so I don't glaze over *that* much."

"Those are Johnny-come-lately compared to her."

"Is Aniko a friend who you could call in need? Like, now?"

"One hundred percent!"

My mom began to fiddle with her watch, which was driving me crazy.

"Please stop playing with your watch."

"Oh, fuck off, Joel. I can do whatever I want."

"When you returned from the war, did she know what had happened to you? Have you ever talked about the war since then? Did she understand what happened to you?" I wanted to know.

"Of course, she knew. The book her husband just wrote is called *The Fourth Passenger*; the protagonist is a Holocaust survivor. And, if I wouldn't have to waste my time on podcasting, I would have more time to read it."

"How often do you speak to her?"

"Almost never."

We both laughed. But my mom made it clear that they write to each other often and stay in close touch thanks to Mark Zuckerberg and Facebook.

I barely knew three-quarters of my Facebook "friends," which made me wonder how my mom defines a meaningful friendship.

"There are different types of friendships that I had through my life. All sorts of different types. Some I just have, and I'm not even sure why. I am a royal bullshitter, and I truly enjoy the repartee of a friendship. So, I always had those types of friends in life. And then, I have what I describe as good weather friends, who only seem to show up only when things are going well. And then, I have friends that I can count on in very bad weather, no matter the conditions, like Rita."

"So, I don't want to ostracize you from certain friends because of this book, but if I had to put you on the spot right now and say who is your best friend in the world, who would you say it is?"

"I would say Rita."

"You're supposed to say your husband!" I exclaimed.

"I love Roy most in the world. Unfortunately, he's basically a vegetable now at Miami Jewish."

She looked sad, understandably, but quickly regained her focus.

"I really value the whole concept of friendship so much. It is probably one of the things that is most important to me. I love the idea of loyalty because I come from a part of Yugoslavia where loyalty was a very important thing culturally. It kind of weaved itself through the culture. People took pride in being honorable. Honor was very important and not something to be messed with in any way. Strong friendships were part of this code. The Serbs consider close friends just like brothers or sisters. Friendship carries the same weight as family. So, it's very important, and that's how I grew up and why I'm still good friends with someone like Aniko Botka."

My mom remains fiercely loyal to all her friends, and now I have a better sense of why. She continued to hammer her point home.

"I think that friendship really enriches life. It's one of the great things this world has to offer. I work on my friendships. I cultivate them by doing little things to keep them going."

"Like, what do you do to keep a friendship strong?"

"Well, with the ones who are still alive, and that number is quickly dwindling, I call them often. I am truly curious to hear how they are doing. I listen to their stories, and I expect them to listen to mine. We get each other's jokes."

"How have you maintained some of these friendships for close to eighty years or even more with people like Aniko Botka?"

"Aniko and I, like I told you, were friends as babies in our diapers. But Ksenjia Petrovic, for example, I met her after eighth grade. We've made a conscious effort to remain friends."

"Why are you staring at me?" I asked.

"You have way too much facial hair. It's unkempt and white, and it looks like shit. Please shave."

This was a recurring critique. I looked through her like a pane of glass, which is something she taught me to do to others when they were aggravating.

"Where do you rank friendships next to children and family, by the way?" I wanted to make sure I was still more important than all these people whose names she was dropping.

"I rank the importance of these friendships right after you," my mom answered, giving me a goofy look knowing I was looking for this precise answer.

"Selfishly, what do *you* get out of all these friendships?"

"I have an answer for you. I—I feel like we are fellow travelers in this world in a symbolic way. Imagine a road, and you're traveling together on this road, which I know sounds cliché, but we really are traveling together on this road called 'life,' and we have all these shared experiences."

"By the way, my belly fat is almost gone," I mentioned as a non sequitur. I get a sick, twisted pleasure from switching subjects on my mom, especially when she's explaining something important. I always get a rise out of her. Would I ever grow out of this immaturity? It was payback for the facial hair comment she just flung at me.

"You could lose some more." My mom often won these battles involving my boyish behavior.

"You think I look strong?" I asked after proudly spending three weeks in the gym.

"You look massive, man."

"So, tell me when you first met Rita and how you knew this would be a long-lasting friendship, your best friend as you say?"

"We met at the Maison Juive at the University of Geneva, the same place I met your father, but I met Rita before Dad. It was 1959, and I was commuting forty minutes by train back and forth from my Uncle George's house."

"What does your forty-minute commute have anything to do with this?"

"Well, I'm getting to it. If you had any patience, you'd know this. I had no social life because of the commute, and I had no money. I wanted to live on my own at the university. So, I asked around, and someone told me I should meet this young woman named Rita Feuerstein, which was her maiden name."

"I'm trying desperately to care about this. I'm falling asleep. But go on."

"Screw you, then. I don't need you to care. You asked a question, and I'm answering it now!"

"Can you speed it up a bit? I have to go get the kids soon."

"Well, maybe if I didn't speak six languages and wasn't eighty-four years old, I'd be a little faster. It takes me longer to process my thoughts now, and you're a bitch."

We laughed, and I reminded my mom that I'm recording everything. She proclaimed her innocence and said if I tried to paint her as an old expletive-spewing woman no one would believe me. People routinely asking her to bless them poolside at her building was beginning to go to her head.

"Anyway, Rita was renting a room from Ms. Bonk on Sixty-Three Rue du Lobar. I was nineteen, and so was Rita. She was studying architecture, and we decided we were going to split the rent. We had use of the kitchen."

"Do you think she's dead now?"

"Who?"

"Ms. Bonk."

"Are you an idiot? Are you just trying to annoy me? This was 1959, and she must've been seventy-five then. No, she's alive and giving ice skating lessons in Geneva. You'll eventually grow up, or maybe you never will."

I laughed out loud. The original LOL.

"Anyway, we moved in together. And this is how our friendship began."

She was back to fiddling with her watch. But I decided I'd ignore it and not give my mom the pleasure of knowing how much it irritated me. She continued the story of the first days of her friendship with Rita.

"We'd always speak late at night. We shared a room with our beds in an L-shape, and we'd just talk and talk. One night, she told me her whole life story. It's one of the few times we ever spoke about the war. But we had so much in common, and I said to Rita, 'You are stealing my life story.' We cried. No one ever really understood us until this moment. And now we had each other."

"What did she tell you?"

"She was born in Poland, and her father was also killed by the Nazis. Her mother also remarried like Grandma Anyu. And Rita also had a half sister like me. She also told me about her dreams to become a successful architect, which she did and then some."

"I mean, it's so crazy that she was hidden in a large coffin at night with her mother." I still had trouble believing this was true, but sadly it was.

"It was much worse in Poland, but, still, we were like almost the same. We were almost the same."

My mom had that look like she was about to tell me something upsetting.

"The big difference was that when she was about six years old, her family moved to Israel. So, she grew up in Israel. She served in the Israeli army. And she was tough, but I was tough too."

It always ate away at my mom that she didn't raise her family in Israel. She was kicked out of her childhood home and always yearned for the security of her own homeland. It's something I could never relate to growing up in America with great television and football, basketball, and baseball. It's why my mom still loves to call me a "dumb American."

"Not soon after we met Buria, and the three of us were inseparable."

Bruria was my mom's other very close friend. She was also born in Poland, forced to live in heinous conditions during the war, eventually becoming one of the top female attorneys in the State of Israel. She died about a decade ago of cancer, and I vividly remembered how crushed my mom was to get that terrible news. I asked her how she was different than Rita.

"With Rita you can never sit down in a cafe and shoot the breeze. She's hyper and always must do something. She's a very talented painter and even better architect. Her mind was always moving so fast. Bruria and I could just sit and bullshit for hours. She's everything I am, but she much smarter and so fast and witty."

"How long did it take before you two shared your stories of survival?"

"It was almost immediate. The minute we both found out the other was Jewish and from Eastern Europe, we knew. Like Rita, Bruria was from Poland too. Her father was the equivalent of a superior court judge."

My mom told me to turn off the recorder. She told me there were parts of Bruria's story that she didn't want to share. I asked why, and she told me it was none of my business. But I can unequivocally tell you that many survivors, including my dear mother, retreat into irrational paranoia sometimes. They prefer to keep parts of their stories private and sacred. And who am I to judge?

"Bruria's story was different. She was taken care of by a peasant family in the country. She was there for years, not months, by herself. Her mother was hiding somewhere, and her father was hiding in a different place. By the end of the war, she was so confused because she felt like a member of the family who was hiding her. They were Gentiles, and Bruria struggled with that too, with her own identity. The war affected people in so many ways so many don't understand."

Wow, this thought had never occurred to me. How could my mother and I be only one generation apart? I was scrolling through my X feed unable to compute that my own mom had to hide in a city that only had horses and buggies to get around. How could so much change so soon? And could the life of comfort I was so accustomed to living end as swiftly and senselessly as hers did? She continued to tell me about Bruria.

"As I just said, Bruria was raised by a Gentile family, so she felt very Gentile. It was very hard for her to return to Judaism, even though she also moved to Israel."

"In 1999, on Michael Moore's advice, I interviewed the three of you. And what was interesting to me is that you guys had never since college, I guess, never really spoke about the past. Why don't you think you guys dwelled on your stories of survival more? In fact, you didn't seem to discuss it at all. Why?"

"I think all three of us, at that point, were moving forward in life. Like I said, Bruria became a brilliant and very successful attorney. We had started interpreter school together. Her mother tongue was Polish, and she lived in Israel, but she still took notes in French much faster than me. She was so smart, and her mind was so fast. It was hard to keep up."

"Who was the smartest of the three of you?"

"We were all smart but in different areas. I think I was the smartest about life, and I can definitely declare this now because Bruria is dead and Rita is eight thousand miles away in Israel. I hope she doesn't read this."

"What makes you the smartest about life?"

"I found true happiness with your father. They both struggled in that department, even though they were both married too."

My mom tried to get me to stop the recording again because she wanted to amend what she had just said. I told her I have strong journalistic ethics and integrity, and there was no going back. She tried to rip the phone out of my hand. But my reflexes were no match for hers. She was annoyed but continued.

"Rita met someone who wasn't Jewish, and she didn't want to upset her mom. And it's none of your business, so I'm going to leave it at that."

"So, moving on, you've had a lot of friends and a lot of different sorts of friends. Why do you think people gravitate to you?"

From the earliest days of my existence, at least from the days I can remember, my mom has had some sort of magnetic attraction. People love her and want to be in her circle. Somehow, she draws in the most eclectic mix of humans one can imagine.

"I always had a lot of interesting friends. I think I'm fun and engaged in what they all have to say. But not everyone likes me. Some people get me; others don't. There are a lot of people in my building who totally don't get me for some reason."

She gets hounded by flocks of people in her building, so I wasn't sure what she was telling me now. Was my poor mom looking for comfort and reassurance? Was she feeling lonely with my dad now living at Miami Jewish?

"I guess I'm a weird person. Like I'm not a snob, but in some ways, I am a snob. I don't need designer handbags or designer clothes, so I'm not a snob in that sense of the word. But education is very important to me, so sometimes I snap if people are too slow or not clever enough or fast or funny enough."

"So, you are a snob!"

We laughed.

"You can't be too much of a snob if you were friends with Jerry for all those years." I comforted my mom.

Jerry's real name was Jorgovanka Miljkovic. More than forty years ago, my mom was introduced to her in our hometown of Highland Park, New Jersey. She had emigrated from Serbia and cleaned houses for a living, including ours. Jerry was probably the hardest-working person I'd ever met. She cleaned all day and worked the graveyard shift at a local factory. Over time, she built J.M. Cleaning Services into a small empire, despite never even graduating from elementary school. My mom and Jerry developed an impenetrable friendship, which included a deep love for each other. Jerry never missed a Waldman family event, attending bar mitzvahs, high school and college graduations, and weddings. And you could be sure as the day is long that Jerry gave you the most generous gift, putting others before herself. Sadly, Jerry died of terminal cancer a few years ago, which some attribute to her work in the factory. We all loved Jerry and still do, but especially my mom.

"Why were you such good friends with Jerry? She couldn't have been more different than you. She had zero education and was basically illiterate. You were both from Serbia, but in reality, you were from two different worlds."

"Jorgovanka had natural intelligence. You know, without any formal education, she was still one of the smartest people I knew and, also, a very decent person. She was very honorable to me. She was also fiercely loyal and would do anything for me, and I would do anything for her. Our friendship was based on mutual loyalty. It was based on our common language too. There was something about the fact that I could use this language that I studied for eighteen years. All the books I read as a child were in Serbian, and here was this woman in Highland Park who understood me, and we would jabber away for hours."

"I thought you just admitted to being a snob. There was literally no one more uneducated than Jerry."

"Sometimes I am, sometimes I'm not. And just because you're not formally educated doesn't mean you're not smart and can't still be a great friend. It's exactly the opposite. In many ways, she understood me better than anyone else. I really admired how she made a life for herself in America."

"Yes, but my point is that she was from a totally different world than you. So, what do you think made you guys gravitate toward each other?

"It's a good question. I don't really know the answer, but I think it's all the things I just mentioned. We had a common language, and I genuinely respected her too."

"Do you think you felt like you wanted to help her because she also had an abusive husband?"

Jerry's husband, Bogoljub Miljkovic, would occasionally get physical. My mother would find out and threaten him by saying she'd call the police. My mom took the abuse personally and would lash out at him in Jerry's defense. As a kid, I remember my mom getting right up in his face and wagging her finger at him. My mom is fearless in that way.

"He was a prick. A real son of a bitch" is all my mom had to say about Jerry's husband, who passed away a few years before her. "By the way, Jerry still owes me fifteen thousand dollars, which I loaned her, and she promised she'd pay it back. I guess that's never happening."

"How would you describe your relationship with Janet Sichel?"

If you searched the globe for someone more different than Jerry, you might find Janet. Originally from Clark, New Jersey, Janet had moved to Israel in the late 1960s, where she met my mom. She's super high energy with an equally high IQ and a thick Jersey accent, which I loved. My fondest memory of Janet is her making Sam and Mickey, her sons, and me scrambled eggs with ketchup.

"I love Janet with all my heart. Our friendship was very fun and enjoyable. We like the same things. We laugh at the same things."

"How come you just described your friendship in the past tense?"

"Because I think we are getting ready to die. We're both bored by life already. Bored by life," my mom repeated, realizing she didn't intentionally mean to put their friendship in the past while they still had life ahead of them, albeit who knew how much.

"Did you two immediately get each other?"

"Yes, because there is so much humor. We can't go two seconds without laughing. But, unlike Jerry, she's also the type of a person who will never do anything for you!"

My mom looked at my phone, which I now kept at a distance too far for her to try to snatch it.

"Do not dare put that in the book!" she laughed. "I keep forgetting you're recording all of this. Goddamn it."

"I'm definitely putting it in. I've given you so many warnings already."

"Well, what I mean is she's not the type of friend who is going to offer to clean your oven or something." My mom was in damage-control mode.

"She's very, very smart. She worked as a copyright editor. And she was always so much more clever than everyone around her. She never did much with it, but she's still so creative."

"Okay, Mom, you don't have to kiss her ass. She'll probably never even read this because, like you just said, she's only really focused on Janet."

"I never said that! I just said she wouldn't be the first to raise her hand to clean my oven. Janet is so much fun. We could spend an afternoon together and just never stop cracking up." My mom smiled wide as she reminisced about one of her few friends who still somehow managed to stay alive.

"Janet, Rita, and Bruria all knew each other. Do you think it was your collective intelligence which helped create the special bond you all have still, except poor Bruria who left us?"

"No, no. We are smart. But humor is what brought us all together. We would all try to outdo each other. It was like an ongoing competition to show who was the most funny, clever, and witty. And I think it was me! Different friendships have different chemistry, and when we were all together, it was beautiful and easy."

My mom recently attended her fifty-fifth high school reunion in Subotica. Her closest friend from those days, besides Aniko Botka, is Ksenjia Petrovic, whose last name I never knew until now. I'll say it again: it's amazing what you learn when you write a book about your mom. You realize how much you still don't know about the person closest to you in life.

"When did you first meet Ksenjia?"

The few things I knew about Ksenjia is that she lived in Las Vegas, got divorced years ago, raised llamas at one point, and was now dangerously thin weighing less than ninety pounds, which of course worried my mom.

"In eighth grade, Ksenjia came to our school, and I started to talk to her. And we were just on the same wavelength. She's also very, very smart. But she's not funny. She gets into real dark moods. She's withdrawn from the world now and very depressed. Ksenjia had a very hard life."

"What made it so hard? And do you feel, because you're a therapist, that you can save her?"

"She wasn't Jewish, so she never hid. But her parents divorced, and then her dad died suddenly. And, while she might look like an elderly woman now, these things stick with you for life. She could never escape it. She became a schoolteacher and got divorced herself, and then raised her only daughter all alone. She became very bitter. And to answer your last question, no! I'm not in the business of saving people anymore."

I'm not sure if I believe my mom. Her nature is to help people, and I don't think that instinct ever leaves you, no matter how long you've been retired or how old you are.

"What about all your friends from Highland Park like Susan Feldman, Marilyn Lerner, and Barbara Glitzer?" All three had died over the last ten years or so.

"I knew Susan before either of us had children."

Susan's son Rob and I were inseparable as young boys. He's arguably the smartest person ever to live. I remember him doing physics problems with his Grandpa Jack in second grade. He could've done anything he wanted but ultimately went into finance, where he made boatloads of money before also dying of cancer at just fifty-one. Rob definitely got the money memo. I told you he was smart.

"How was your friendship with Susan Feldman?" I asked, realizing how different our perception of relationships is as children compared to adults. Innocence is truly bliss.

"It was a little complicated, but I liked her a lot. Why you will ask. Because she was also funny and smart as hell. And quirky too."

For some reason, I still remember the first time we ever knocked on the Feldman's door. Susan answered the door with these trippy-looking cat-eye glasses. I'd like to say they were stylish, but they were just sort of odd. She looked like she jumped off a 1970s blacklight poster.

"She was funny and quirky. One of the things that intrigues me about people and friendships revolve around psychology. It was my profession for a reason. I'm still drawn to what makes a person tick. She had an interesting background, and I found her intriguing, and I think that's why we remained friends for close to sixty years."

It was strange to reminisce about all these friends whom I knew well too, who were now also all gone. It seems like our mortality comes into sharper and sharper focus with each passing day until we become those friends others speak about in the past tense.

"What's it like to lose all these close friends? How do you cope with it?"

"Much easier than with my husband's impending death. I'm not sure I'll survive that. *Surviving the Survivor* may become more than just the title of our podcast and this book when that happens," she told me with a wry smile.

"Dad will be okay," I tried to reassure her, sounding about as convincing as a used car salesman.

"Well, some deaths are harder than the others. Losing Susan was difficult because she was so young, only in her seventies."

For my mom, now eighty-four, it was an incomprehensibly young age for a person to be taken.

"Susan went through a lot of tragedy for somebody who never even went through the Holocaust. Both her brothers died much younger than her, and she took it very, very hard. Each death devastated her worse than the other. And Arthur, her sweet husband, died young too. I think it may have had something to do with the water in that part of New Jersey; she was raised right next to the filthy Passaic River."

"Whose friend's death has been the toughest for you to handle?"

"It's Bruria for sure but ask me tomorrow because it could change quickly with so many people dying now." My mom tried to make light of the ultimate outcome of aging.

"I loved hanging out with Bruria. I mean, she could be a pain in the ass and complained a lot, but look, she was already diagnosed with cancer in her early thirties. She went through so much, from the war to being very sick."

My mom was back to fiddling with her watch, trying to distract herself from the painful reality that she was one of the few remaining of her once big circle of friends. The circle was morphing into a triangle.

"Friendships are something that I put at a premium. I spend a lot of time and energy on my friendships because anything that's worth its salt in life takes tremendous work. I don't drop friends because they're too far away or even if they complain too much. Instead, I double down, and I try to be okay with my friends."

"Do you ever get to an age where you get tired of the effort it takes to maintain some of these friendships?"

"I don't have too many friends left to exert that much energy. But, no, I don't think I'll ever get to a point where I don't want to meet friends anymore. I just need to pick younger ones," she joked again, but the pain underneath was real.

"You think it's just human nature that we all crave friendships?"

"Not necessarily because there are different types of people. We're both extroverts, but there are also plenty of introverts who probably prefer to have far fewer friends. And both are fine. To each his own."

"What would life be like without great friends?"

"It would suck even if you didn't have great friends and just mediocre ones," she laughed, but meant it. "I love Fran Malkin, but Fran ditches me the minute her daughter calls, and I do the same when you call, so you have to accept all these caveats in these friendships."

Fran is also a survivor. They met fairly recently in New Jersey.

"I must say that I like, like I have, like what's her name is coming on the nineteenth, Friday the nineteenth. Um, um…"

"Spit it out!" I screamed. I noticed my mom having some more "senior moments" these days, which always tested my nerves. She called them "senior moments," not me, to be clear.

"Charlotte Schwartz?" I asked. She was one of the few friends I knew my mom had in south Florida.

"Yes, Charlotte Schwartz. She is coming soon. Charlotte Schwartz. I like her, but she's like…"

I felt generous and reminded my mom once again that I was recording our entire conversation. She looked down at my cell phone again.

"Never mind then," she said sheepishly.

"You're going to have a lot less friends *after* this book is published," I reassured her jokingly.

The paranoia of being outed hit her hard.

"No, no, no, no, no, no, no. But you can't say certain things, Joel. Joel, you can't do this. If you do this, I'll kill you. You'll destroy my life. I forgot I'm being taped," she pleaded to no avail, as I tauntingly shook the cell phone in front of her.

"How would you sum up the importance of friendship?"

"Your OCD is kicking in. How many times are you going to ask me basically the same exact thing in just a slightly different way? I told you I feel very strongly that it's one of the wonderful things that life offers. But each of us bears the responsibility to try to make the friendship work."

"How so?"

"Like I said, for the third time now, you must cultivate it. You can't just assume that a friendship will bloom on its own.

And it helps to be in the same place at the same time because technology only carries you so far."

"Anything else? This is a book, not an article."

"Oh f…"

My mom was about to drop the f-bomb but looked down at my phone and thought better of it. She's learning, even at eighty-four.

"I think you shouldn't expect too much from friendships, in general, because then you're going to end up disappointed."

A classic move by my mom, dropping a bomb on everything she had previously told me, just as we were wrapping up this part of the conversation.

"What do you mean by that?"

"I mean, if you expect a friend to always be there for you and to always do the right thing and to never do anything to aggravate you, then you'll end up disappointed."

"Does dropping dead count as disappointment?"

"Yes, and too many of my friends have done exactly that!"

"Well at least those friends won't be mad at you for anything you say in this book," I said as I waved the cell phone in her face again.

"Fuck off, Joel, don't you dare print anything nasty."

Actual Voicemail from My Mom: *July 25, 2022*

I just canceled Dr. Ciment's appointment for tomorrow.

Dad is doing well. He's not coughing. Arden and I and Anna, we thought maybe he doesn't really need to go.

Anyway, we have no appointment for tomorrow, so I just wanted to let you know as you're planning your day.

This is your mother, by the way.

"I'LL BE DEAD SOONER THAN LATER"

"No, I'm not doing it!"

"I produce the podcast, and all you do is show up."

My mom and I argued every Friday like clockwork. This week was no different.

Instead of discussing aging, a topic I knew she was desperately trying to avoid, she was perturbed I planned a lower-profile story for the podcast she co-hosts with me Sunday evenings.

Since we pivoted to true crime all the time after the horrific quadruple murders in Moscow, Idaho, our numbers skyrocketed with roughly one hundred thousand YouTube subscribers and over two million views some months. Along with our soaring viewership, my mom's ego was inflating just as fast. I dubbed her "the Diva."

"You give me the shit stories on Sunday nights, and our numbers are a fraction of what you get when you host solo!" she screamed.

"Are you fucking kidding me?"

She was smiling at me, but I wish I could say she was joking. She wasn't. I was incredulous.

"This Utah mom accused of poisoning her husband is everywhere; it's a huge story." I worked to quell her frustration.

"Your shows get five times what mine get on Sunday night." She was unrelenting. She now co-hosts with me every Wednesday. It became too much for me to host a live show six nights a week.

"Mom, you're eighty-four. Your husband is in Miami Jewish, which is basically a waiting room for the cemetery. I was kind enough to move here with my kids. Not only do you have your grandchildren, but I'm single-handedly turning you into YouTube celebrity with very little time left on your clock. So, are you being serious right now?"

"Do I look like I'm joking?"

"I'm going to call you out on the show Sunday night!"

"Don't you dare!"

My mom, affectionately known as Karm on *Surviving the Survivor*, is becoming a cult of personality. There are nights when she trends on social media because STS Nation, as our community is known, is so obsessed with her. She's smart, funny, and sharp as hell for a woman halfway through her eighties. She can also be a pain in the ass to work with.

"Do you have anything else to say before we discuss your favorite topic: aging?"

"Yes."

"What?"

"Buy low and sell high."

"Speaking of buying low and selling high, Littman says he can get me that Omega watch at cost."

I knew this would set her off. It was payback for annoying me about her show topics on Sunday nights.

"What? What?"

She wanted to know if she correctly heard what I had just said. Michael Littman is one of my best friends, whose family had been in the jewelry business for generations. Mike, owner of Manalapan, New Jersey's Gary Michael's Fine Jewelers, would get us good deals on watches, even though the cheap bastard would make you split the cost of a Carvel milkshake right down the middle with him.

"Littman can get me that Omega Speedmaster watch I love at just above cost. I've been kissing his ass to get the price down."

"Why don't you become a male prostitute?" she asked rhetorically.

"It's a beautiful watch. It has a green alligator band with a green face. It's beautiful!"

"How much?"

"It retails for twenty-eight thousand dollars, but Littman can get it for me for around twenty even."

"What? What?"

Two "whats" in a row was my mom's telltale signature of annoyance. When she hit two in a row, back-to-back, I knew I had succeeded in riling her up.

"Oh my god, you're so pathetic. I'm not talking to you about something as stupid as a watch!"

Our stare down was on.

"Did I really raise you to be this stupid? Are you this much of a hollow head? A watch? For twenty thousand dollars? For what? So, you can show off?"

She straightened out her own wristwatch, which was twisted up.

"I got this for three thousand dollars on my fiftieth wedding anniversary. I cannot believe you whine about money and talk about buying a twenty-thousand-dollar Omega watch. I must've failed as a mother."

She may have failed as a mother, but I was succeeding as a son at driving her crazy. And I'm getting that watch. I'll just keep it quiet.

"Can we start?" I asked.

"I could spit on you, I'm so aggravated!"

"Well, take a deep breath. Is youth wasted on the young as the cliché goes?" We began our discussion about aging. She looked down at her watch and collected herself.

"One of the things I observed is that life is really like traveling through time. When you're young, you're not expected to have life experience. So, you do the best with what you have at that time."

She abruptly stopped speaking.

I wondered why.

"Are you taping?" she asked.

"Yes, I'm recording. Let me worry about producing, just like the podcast, Mom."

"Well, in your youth, you have a limited number of experiences. And then as you travel through life, you accumulate more and more experiences. It doesn't make you wiser, but you are familiar with more that comes your way. But it doesn't necessarily mean you make better choices later in life."

"When you look in a mirror now, does it compute with what you see in the mirror?"

"No, absolutely not."

"Can you please elaborate? Three-word answers aren't particularly riveting for the reader."

"Well, I just read some scientists predict that in 2050 there is a danger that the skyscrapers in New York City could be underwater. There are fears now that they're too heavy for the island they stand on. But, I'm thinking, wait a minute, I won't physically be around in 2050. But I don't feel this way mentally. It's a very strange thought."

In that instant, I got super sad thinking about the harsh reality of my mom being gone forever. Who would I annoy about buying a watch? I couldn't allow myself to think about it.

I had just been sent a meme that read, "When your mom is no longer here, you'll realize you lost your only true friend." A tear welled up in my eye.

"It doesn't feel real," my mom continued, "because your brain is simply not wired to process your mortality. I'll be dead sooner than later, but my brain doesn't let me believe this."

Maybe aging was a topic to avoid? It was too late now. We were in it.

"Your brain is even less capable of processing finality when you are young. Our time in this life is so incredibly limited. Even Roy, your father, who was very, very smart, only realized later in life that he should worry about the passing of time. He was always more concerned, as we've discussed, about outliving his money. So, back to your question, every morning when I look in the mirror, I'm a little bit surprised and concerned at what I see."

"When you look in the mirror, what do you see?"

"I see a very wrinkled, hunched-over little lady. That's all I see."

I laughed from nervousness. My mom who was always so beautiful, and still is in my eyes, aged considerably—and even more jarring—seemingly very quickly.

"So, that's what you see? But what do you feel like?"

"I feel like I could move mountains. On the inside, I don't feel at all how I look on the exterior. Part of the reason, thank

God, is I've never really been sick. Many people my age have arthritis or Parkinson's. I've been so lucky so far."

"When I was getting a haircut today, there was a woman there that was..."

"You got a haircut? I looked at you, but I didn't realize until this moment that you got a haircut!"

"Well, then pay attention!" I told her.

My mom, a therapist by trade, was always people watching, so curious about us humans and why we act the way we do. I inherited this trait. That's why I was amazed at what I witnessed while getting my haircut earlier in the day.

"This woman, she had to be over a hundred years old. She had this horribly dyed red hair and fake eye lashes that jumped out at you. She sort of reminded me of Helen Thomas."

"Who is Helen Thomas?"

"She's that White House reporter. She was so old she covered George Washington," I joked. "And then she got in trouble for saying, 'Jews should get the hell out of Palestine!'"

"Oh, yes, I remember," my mom added, without missing a beat. "She should've died sooner, that anti-Semite."

My mom has a zero-tolerance policy for anyone who is anti-Israel or anti-Semitic in any way, shape, or form. The current war in Israel exacerbated all those feelings.

"This woman," I continued. "She had to be one hundred and five. And she was preening her hair like a peacock does its feathers, staring at herself in the mirror, and just admiring everything about herself, including her outrageous eyebrows and pancake makeup, which was red to match her thinning hair."

"She was probably seventy," my mom interrupted. "The sun does that to you here in Florida."

"Trust me, she was way older than you," I assured my mom, "but, explain to me, at that age, why even bother—why care at that age?"

"This reminds me of when we used to take your Uncle Alan, may he rest in peace, to his card club. The women there were always dressed to the ninth, tenth—what's the expression?"

"It's actually elevens," I joked. "No, maybe it's thirteens. It's dressed to the nines!"

"Dressed to the nines. That's it!" She was excited to get it right. "The women there were always so dressed up with all their jewelry, makeup, hair perfectly coiffed, and beautiful outfits. They always bothered to make an effort. And they didn't even have men to dress up for. All their husbands had already croaked. They dressed up just to dress up."

"So, what's that all about? Is it ego? What is it?" I was genuinely curious why they even bothered at this point.

"No, it's not ego. Maybe a little bit. But I think it's also like an ingrained habit to just get up in the morning and do your thing."

"But do you think these women still see themselves as beautiful in their own minds?"

"I have no idea how they see themselves. I know I see myself as old when I look in the mirror. Bottom line. But I was never one to lie to myself."

"Does it upset you?"

"No. What upsets me is that I won't be here soon to see myself still aging."

"When did you realize your own mortality? That you had an expiration date?" I was curious as I had never really pondered my own mortality until very recently. My mom's answer surprised me, which is really no surprise at all.

"When I was four years old."

"Elaborate, please. Don't give me one-word answers. I already told you ten times this is supposed to be a book, not a feature article in the *New Yorker*.

"When I was very, very young, I realized that we are not on this planet forever. At an age when most people I knew believed they'd be around forever, I knew this was not the case. From very early on, I knew I was only here on a temporary basis. And the only way I could counteract that jolting reality in my own head was to enjoy every single day, to find a way to enjoy something every single day. And I still practice this today."

"Do you think your perspective on aging was affected by your experience in the war?"

"Yes, that's definitely part of it. You must understand that after the war, everybody in my hometown of Subotica was crying for years. It wasn't hours or days or weeks; people cried for years. I'm not exaggerating. You couldn't go to services in the synagogue on the high holidays without hearing weeping echoing off the high walls and ceilings. It wasn't a joyous place. Our entire town was overwrought with emotion. I heard endless sobbing, and that takes a toll on you as a young child who knew her own pain from losing her dad. I knew so many other people died besides just my father, and it made me understand, albeit at too young an age, that our time here is but a blink of an eye."

I tried desperately to process what my mom was telling me in that moment, but again I came up empty. In a lot of ways, I felt the way people sometimes describe sociopathic killers who are incapable of feeling. I was completely numb attempting to reconcile my mom's tragic past and her very limited future. So, feeling utterly helpless, I switched gears.

"There's a cliché that 'age is nothing but a number.' Do you subscribe to this?"

"Yes. Sort of. It's true to a point. But when you run up a high number and become eighty-four, then you start to feel your age. And, if you're honest with yourself, you know death isn't too far away."

"So, you consciously feel like your time here on earth is very limited?"

"I feel it every minute of every day now. I feel that in the most realistic sense."

"You do?" This conversation was becoming so depressing.

"I do every minute."

"But just a little while ago, you told me your mind is still sharp and you feel strong, didn't you?"

"Because, as I've told you a million times before, it never matters how you feel. It's the reality of what *is*. The harsh reality is most people, the vast majority of people, if they're lucky enough to make it into their eighties, begin to disintegrate around then."

"Has your perspective on aging evolved over the years?"

"In life, you need to know yourself. And one thing I know to be true about me is I never have really evolved. I have the same political views I had fifty years ago. I have the same views on religion that I had fifty years ago. I have the same views on aging that I had fifty years ago. The way I think about these things hasn't really changed. I'm a decisive and stubborn person. So, what I thought then is what I still think now."

My mom, I think, was being a bit hyperbolic. I've seen her change some over the years. For one, she has less patience for my bullshit.

"I actually think I've evolved over the last bunch of months that your father has been in Miami Jewish. Seeing him deteriorate before my eyes, from day to day, makes me realize how irreversible death is. The truth is when he passes I'll never ever see him again."

"You know Jews believe in the *olam ha-ba*, the world to come. Do you feel guilty admitting you're not a believer in this?"

"Do I look like I feel guilty?"

In recent years, my mom and I discussed religion more than ever before. We both confided in the other that we're highly skeptical of much that Judaism offers, most notably an afterlife. It's too difficult for either of us to drum up that much faith. My sister, who is modern Orthodox, seems to believe it all. But my mom and I never quite got there. But what if it is true? Would God keep us out because of our skepticism? I second-guessed myself. My mother never would.

"For some reason, until just months ago, I never grasped that I won't ever see your father again. Maybe my optimism blinded me?" she rhetorically asked.

"You don't feel guilty saying any of this out loud? That you basically deny a major tenet of Judaism?"

"Guilt is an emotion for pussies."

It's amazing my mom didn't drop the p-word earlier in this book. She uses the word "pussy" more than any other woman, let alone an eighty-four-year-old woman that I—or probably you—know.

"I am not a deep thinker. So, I never realized that when it ends, it's over forever and ever."

"Are you afraid of aging now?"

"I was never afraid. And I'm not afraid now. I accept it as an ugly fact of life. Why would I be afraid of it? How can I fight it? What can I do about it?"

"So, you just give into it?"

"No."

"Please don't make me remind you again to not give one-word answers."

"I just live in spite of knowing this."

"But you're a control freak. How are you able to function knowing that you can't control the passing of time?"

"I am accepting of it because nothing can be done to change it. It's like the famous Alcoholics Anonymous quote: 'God, grant me the serenity to accept the things I cannot change, the courage to change the things I can, and the wisdom to know the difference.' I was never an alcoholic, but I love that saying."

I knew my mom would let the world know she never drank. In fact, she had no real vices that I've ever known about, except maybe the tendency to drop f-bombs.

"What's the worst part about aging?"

"The worst part about aging is that you must be prepared to move on to wherever we go next. That's the worst part."

"Well, you just implied you're not going to some heavenly world to come?"

"I don't. And, by the way, Jews believe the world to come only exists for those who truly believe in it. So, I'm screwed either way. Boy, I hope I'm not wrong!"

"Do you feel like you should have more faith? Is it too late to start believing in the world to come?"

"Joel, you can't force these things. You just cannot force it upon yourself. Roy, your poor dad, tried so hard to force himself into believing it. But, in the end, while he was still coherent and cogent, he confessed his doubts."

"And you have no sense of guilt?"

"God should feel guilty for creating death," my mom responded deadpan.

"Does anything positive come with aging?"

"There are very few. But one is that you lower your expectations. You are more accepting of what's coming your way, I think. And you get less worked up about stupid things, except when you aggravate me."

One of my biggest regrets in life is that I shared too much with my mom and put her through too much stress. I know this might be difficult to grasp, but I tend to whine, and I'm sick thinking that could ultimately become my legacy. Was it too late for me to change? Was I aging too fast to reverse course?

"I read somewhere, and I bet it's true," my mom continued her thought, "that people in their eighties are the happiest group because they're just thrilled to still be here participating in life. Now, the few friends I have left just enjoy looking at flowers budding or bees buzzing around."

"Just yesterday, a frog jumped in my path, and I screamed like a little girl," I confessed to my mom.

"What a brave American you are."

"My point is it made me sad because already Dad doesn't have enough cognition to appreciate the fear of a frog jumping across his path in the dark of night."

"There are countless little, beautiful things we all take for granted until we can sense those final years, days, minutes, and seconds unapologetically descending upon us."

"So, does perspective change with age? I'm confused because a moment ago you told me you still have the same religious and political beliefs from fifty years ago?"

"Well, wait a second. I said that I knew that I was going to die when I was very, very young, and I tried to enjoy every single day of my life. That was my only antidote to dying: to enjoy it while I'm still here."

"Mom, I'm recording this. So, I know exactly what you said, so there can't be any revisionist history."

My mom let out a big grunt, which she's been doing on the podcast too lately, and for which I have publicly chastised her. I don't think she quite fully understands podcasting is an intimate experience and grunting can be very distracting. She insists it adds to her character.

"Did you used to grunt as much as this when you were younger?" I asked.

"Well, I have a very dry mouth and—[another grunt]—and I try to clear my throat. I don't grunt." She wanted to make the dry mouth versus grunt distinction very clear.

"Have you become more impatient in your older age?"

"Only for stupid questions about grunting and tantrums for overpriced watches!"

She looked into my soul and continued.

"With stupidity? Yes, I've become more impatient with stupidity."

"Why are you looking directly at me?"

"You're interviewing me, right?"

"Are you implying that I'm stupid?"

"I never ever said you're stupid. Check your recording. No revisionist history, remember? I said I have no tolerance for stupid behavior."

"So, explain what you mean by 'you are more impatient when it comes to stupid behavior.'"

"I mean exactly that. And I don't sweat the small stuff. I do not allow myself to be bogged down by things that are not important to me."

"I happened to see *Dateline* last night. The husband murdered his wife because they were running out of money. He couldn't handle the embarrassment, so he killed his spouse to divert attention from their financial distress. It stressed me out so much, thinking it could happen to me one day, that I sent you and my wife very lengthy texts about it. Neither of you even responded. Why?"

"You don't deserve a response. Spoiled brats don't deserve responses. And so, you didn't get one. And this is exactly what I'm talking about when I mention stupid behavior. Play with yourself instead of your phone, sending idiotic messages in the middle of the night."

"Is this what you mean by impatience in your older age?"

"Yes! I can't take it anymore. Grow up!"

"What else really irritates you? Dad, for example, recently told us he despises the expression 'killing time' because he wished he had more left. Is there anything that really irks you in your older age?"

"Very few things. Very few things."

She stared at me even harder, opening her eyes a little wider. The obvious implication was I was the only one who really irritated her.

"Is it strange that at one point in life you could seduce men because of your good looks and those days are now behind you?"

"I can still do that."

Was she being serious right now? Then she laughed, unable to remain stoic.

"I had a very funny story from yesterday," she began to tell me. "Lisandra, your dad's nurse, came to see me. I invited her down to the café at the building. There was a tremendous rainstorm, so we were the only people sitting there. And then a man came in and ordered a glass of wine. And he asked, 'Are you ladies having a good time?' He was my age. He may have been closer to ninety."

"Are you about to tell me that you got picked up while Dad is on oxygen at Miami Jewish?"

"Wait a second. *Savlanut!*"

Savlanut means patience in Hebrew, and, for some reason, my mom still uses it all the time, despite having left Israel fifty years ago.

"You really got picked up at the bar?"

"No! But it has a funny ending. He asked again, 'Are you ladies having a good time?' Lisandra doesn't speak English, so she had no idea what he was saying and didn't answer. So, I said, 'Yes, we are having a great time.' He asks, 'Is that your granddaughter?' And I said, 'No, this is not my granddaughter. This is the young woman who helps me with my husband at the nursing home.' And then I realized suddenly that he wasn't picking me up. He was trying to pick up Lisandra because she's a beautiful twenty-eight-year-old woman. I just assumed he was hitting on me because we're similar in age. Maybe he was turned off because I mentioned I have a husband?"

"That's probably not it." We both laughed.

My father, who is on his last legs, still musters up the energy to lift his head from the pillow to check out attractive nurses walking by. It happened just the other day. He's not really verbal anymore, so I just gave him a proud pat on the shoulder.

My mom was still fixated on her new man from the restaurant.

"He tells us that he's from Toronto. He has a place in our building, and he comes down occasionally. I looked at him a little bit suspiciously, and he tells us he's originally from India."

"Indian? I thought they only allowed old Jews in your building. I was sure that was part of the condo bylaws," I joked.

"Yes, Indian. I was just as surprised. He comes down alone, and he actually looked very lonely. He would've chit-chatted with us for hours," my mom continued.

"I can't relate," I told my mom arrogantly. "Like Dad, I've always been able to get women. Obviously, Dad didn't act on it..."

"As far as we know," my mom interrupted. "Who knows what we'll discover once he kicks the bucket," she joked.

"Dad and I could always get women our whole lives. It's a fact that men age better. I mean, look at Harrison Ford. He's in his eighties, and he's starring in a movie, and he's still a sex symbol. Is it difficult that women lose their luster at a certain age?" I asked.

"Are you still recording?"

"Yes!"

"Well maybe you shouldn't anymore. Over eighty percent of the people who listen to our podcast are women!"

She thought they'd be turned off by my gender-biased arrogance. My mom made a good point. But this was too fun to stop now.

"Does it suck to lose your sexiness as a woman?"

"Yes, it sucks!" my mom admitted. "But it didn't happen now. It happened forty years ago when I was forty."

We both laughed. At forty, my mom had an oil painting of her commissioned by a New York City artist. It's beautiful, and so is she, and I already called first dibs on it when she's no longer aging, if you get my drift.

"It really happened when you were just forty?" I asked.

"Men begin to lose interest in you when you are forty. Although, your dad never lost interest in me. We were still doing it until just before he was sent to Miami Jewish in an ambulance." My mom tried shocking me, which was next to impossible to do since after so many years, I'd become immune to all of this insanity.

"Well, look at someone like J.Lo—she's still attractive in her fifties. I'm not sure if she'll still be a sex symbol at eighty, but she still has it now," I argued.

"It's also generational. Plus, you know how many things she's had fixed and tightened up? I didn't have anything done! No facelift, no Botox—this is all natural," she exclaimed proudly.

"So, you're calling J.Lo out in this book? I love it! Hopefully, she tweets at you, and I sell one hundred million copies of this book!" I got excited for a minute. Maybe taunting my mom was finally going to pay dividends.

"I think she looks terrific. But she's not happy. I saw a picture of her recently."

"You don't think she and Ben are happy?"

My mom has always loved the movies and the tabloid gossip attached to Hollywood celebrities. She was in deep in her Bennifer theory.

"Ben is bad for her. He's a troubled soul, and she should know better. He's been to rehab how many times? He's a gambler too."

"You're a therapist, so what's your advice to J.Lo?"

"She should know herself at fifty, who she is, where she's going, and who she should be with, and Ben is not the right guy." My mom spoke like she was J.Lo's mother-in-law.

"Katharine Hepburn and Spencer Tracy were a great couple. They were together until he died. She spoke openly about their relationship, and she said when most actresses her age were put out to posture, Spencer was still madly in love with her. J.Lo needs a man like Spencer Tracy."

"What about a man like me?"

"You're too old for her."

"By the way, it's pasture, not posture. Posture is when you bitch that I'm not sitting up straight. Pasture, not posture. Katharine Hepburn was put out to pasture, not posture," I reiterated.

"Whatever, all I know is Spencer Tracy made her feel attractive and appealing and feminine. And your father feels the same way about me. That's how you know you have the right man. J.Lo, I'm afraid, has the wrong man, but, hopefully, I'm wrong."

"Did you ever think that when you came here in 1961 that you would still have an accent sixty years later?"

"Yes, because when I was in interpreter school in Geneva, I took a special class to get rid of my accent. It didn't work then, and it doesn't work now. No matter which language I'm speaking, I have a Hungarian accent."

"Were you self-conscious of it?"

"What? What? No, no, no, no, no. My accent is part of who I am. The people at interpreter school wanted me to sound like I could be from anywhere, which is why I never finished it. No one defines me, and certainly not the idiots running the interpreter school at the University of Geneva."

"Have you ever been self-conscious of your accent?"

"Play the tape back. I just said it is part of who I am. In fact, when I first arrived in America, Zsa Zsa Gabor was a big star. Do you know her?"

"Yes, I live on planet earth, I know Zsa Zsa. She had big boobs."

"All you men are the same. She was also very talented. And she had a thick Hungarian accent just like me," my mom said proudly and defiantly.

It was increasingly becoming more difficult to keep my already ADHD-addled mom on track. She was getting worse with age, speaking of aging issues, so I steered her back to the discussion du jour.

"You mentioned J.Lo getting all this work done. What are your thoughts about plastic surgery and antiaging treatments to preserve one's youthful appearance?"

"I think this is America. And, in America, capitalism still reigns supreme. You can pretty much buy or sell whatever you want, for the most part, and that's what makes this country so great."

"But is it futile to get all this work done? Is it an exercise in futility, like a dog chasing its tail?"

"Absolutely, yes," my mom answered.

"What did I tell you about two-word answers? I can't write a book with two-word answers."

"That phone you're recording with is also a store. The minute your phone is on, people are selling you things. Unfortunately, a lot of women and men think there are quick fixes. I can almost always tell when a woman has had work done, and I don't usually like the way it looks. But that's me. Everyone is free to be."

My mom was beginning to grow weary of this conversation, speaking of her ADHD. She was fiddling with her watch again.

"Can you focus for five minutes?"

"Oh, fuck off, Joel. I am focused. I don't need to stare right at you to be present. Don't tell me what to do," she snapped.

"What are the psychological keys to aging well?" I asked.

"It's back to what I said earlier, about AA: accept what you cannot change and change what you cannot accept. By the way, exercise helps keep you sharp and happy too."

My mom still exercises three to four times a week with a personal trainer. My father was into eating healthy and working out decades before it was *en vogue*, which is why he's probably still here at eighty-nine and a half, albeit in Miami Jewish now.

"The physiological and psychological aspects of human beings are very much connected. If you can walk pain-free, arthritis-free, and free of all that other stuff, you will feel better psychologically. It all goes together."

"Hungarians are famous for their skin creams. Do you use anything to prevent wrinkling?"

"Does it look like I do?" my mom pulled on her sagging neck.

Her skin was beginning to look like that of a shar-pei dog, which doesn't bode well for me.

"I don't use any creams. And I hate to tell you why I don't use anything."

"Why?"

"Because I'm way too lazy to apply all those different creams and ointments. I don't have that sort of discipline. I don't think I ever cared enough, and that's why my skin looks like this!"

"When you look in the mirror, do you see your wrinkles?"

"I see nothing but wrinkles. Just wrinkles. It's why your rotten kids say I remind them of an iguana," she laughed.

"What advice do you have for aging gracefully?"

"Well, for one thing, I feel that I was very lucky and very fortunate that I've had your father around. I don't know what I'd do without him. He gives me support, both physically and mentally. We work out together and do puzzles and watch movies together. This kept us sharp. We also give each other a lot of love. And the real secret is love gets you through life looking better than any creams, Botox, fillers, or plastic surgery. Love is the panacea."

"Any other advice on aging?"

"Yes, your son is getting swim lessons now. It's like swimming. Stop thrashing around, otherwise you could drown. Float on top and be calm. You'll last much longer and won't exhaust yourself in the process," she explained.

It was a funny analogy because I don't think I've ever seen my mom swim. I'm not even sure she can. As a child in Yugoslavia, she once saw a man attacked by a shark and has avoided the water ever since.

"Make sure that your brain is occupied with positive things and pleasant things. I know you don't believe me, but our podcast gives me something, a structure for my mind. I read up on all these high-profile crime stories. I think about questions to ask our guests. I read the books that people send us. I try to talk to people who are interesting and who pique my interest.

And I truly enjoy my grandchildren. Just hearing from them keeps me young at heart and slows the aging process."

"Anything else?"

"Yes, one more thing."

"What?"

"It's an absolute fucking myth that you get wiser with age or gain better perspective on life after going through something like the Holocaust! I had to figure out my way through this world just like everyone else. I'm no different."

"Well, this admission ought to really help book sales. You've basically just told every potential reader, 'Don't read this because I know nothing!'"

"Well, it's true."

Actual Voicemail from My Mom: January 23, 2022

Great job, Jo-el,

I just finished watching the podcast. You know I love to watch my performance! And yours too, of course.

[Fumbles phone]

Oy. Bye.

It's your mother, by the way.

"STRAIGHT OUTTA THE NURSING HOME"

Dame Judi Dench, who won the coveted Oscar for *Shakespeare in Love,* didn't find fame until she was sixty years old. It took Morgan Freeman fifty-two years to achieve success. Rodney Dangerfield, whose real name is Jacob Cohen, never got any real respect until he was fifty-nine.

It's taken Karmela Waldman longer than all of them.

She became an unlikely part of YouTube's zeitgeist at eighty-three, making headlines as one of the oldest podcast co-hosts in the country and the only Holocaust survivor we know of regularly helming a show. And it's all thanks to one person—me—her son. I knew she had the so-called "it factor," and after roughly two years behind the microphone, others discovered my mom had the "skills to pay the bills" too, despite already being retired for over twenty years. She was featured on local and national shows and interviewed for a wide variety of both print and digital publications. Her star is still rising rapidly at eighty-four, which she never expected or thought possible.

"Do you remember our first guest?" I asked as we found ourselves back in her kitchen reminiscing about the unlikely success of *Surviving the Survivor,* which now has over one hundred thousand subscribers and well over ten million downloads.

"This is funny and needs to be mentioned!" she told me emphatically. She was about to tell me something she thought was too important to skirt past.

I reminded her that's why I came prepared with my iPhone recorder, all set to further enmesh her fame in this book. She loved the attention, especially knowing her clock was ticking deep into life's fourth quarter. It's also why producer extraordinaire Steve Cohen and I continue to affectionately call her "the Diva."

"You came up with this clever name, *Surviving the Survivor*. You wanted our first show to be all about my Holocaust story, but I refused. I ruled against it because I thought it would be too depressing. Remember, we were also right in the middle of COVID at that time, and I didn't want to bring people down even further. Our audience needed something uplifting, so I talked about how I met your father," she proudly recounted.

At the onset, we were obviously struggling to book high-profile guests as evidenced by our first one ever: my mom.

"It's interesting you bring up the pandemic, Mom. We began the show in January of 2021, which was really the height of COVID and all the paranoia attached to it. So, what was it like for you at that time when we started because, basically, we were still on lockdown?"

"Well, as you know, the swimming pool is sort of the center of social activity in my building, and it was closed. You couldn't even sit outside. I'd look out my window into the parking area, and all I saw was a sea of testing stations. And, early in the morning, I'd see trucks bringing in food for people. It was very dystopian and depressing as hell."

Memories are short. I had already forgotten about so much my mom was describing. We were masked virus avoiders eschewing one another in an effort to sidestep corona, all in the hopes of living to see another day, as fear permeated our collective consciousness more fiercely than any virus ever could.

"Your dad always loves to say, 'Better boredom than suffering.' But I hate boredom. The podcast was my ticket out of the nursing home, which is what I call my condo. We only did the show one day a week back then, but I really looked forward to it. You'd pick me up, both with our masks on, at two thirty p.m. every Wednesday, and we'd head to the studio."

"We even made shirts and coffee mugs that read, 'Straight Outta the Nursing Home'!" I reminded her. "We did it all as a joke, never thinking that one day we'd have an actual online merchandise store where STS Nation buys swag with you on it, Mom!"

A lot of people ask me about the podcast's title. It's something I came up with on a whim, and it stuck. We had never really discussed the name until now.

"What's your understanding of *Surviving the Survivor?*"

"Like most things, it evolves. But I think you perceived me as the person you need to survive because I'm a tough cookie and I don't let you, you know, bullshit me to death. You know you can't manipulate me that much. You can more than most, but it's still hard for you."

My mom decided, like so many other times before, she was going to hijack this interview, metamorphizing into the interviewer before my eyes.

"Remember our original logo?" she asked.

Our logo now is an image of my mother and me smiling. My mom's wearing sunglasses to underscore her "coolness" with an explicit warning label covering her mouth, emphasizing her predilection for profanity. The original logo was way crazier and a lot more controversial.

"I came up with this brilliant idea," she remarked, laughing, "which was stupid, like really stupid, because I had this idea of re-creating the famous image of *Madonna and Child.*"

I had already forgotten the details about this logo origin story. But clearly my mom hadn't.

"Instead of Madonna's face, it was mine. The baby had your face superimposed on it, and you're wearing a diaper with a Knicks jersey, which was all fitting, if it wasn't so outrageous. You were baby Jesus. I mean, you're still my baby."

"I took your vision and ran with it, Mom. I paid good money to have that logo designed by Doug Miller's wife and then you chickened out, why?"

"Joel, you know I'm paranoid. I was afraid Gentiles in our audience would be very offended, even though we had no viewers or listeners back then. I didn't want anyone to think it was a put-down. It was meant to put you down for believing you're like Jesus coming back to earth to save the masses. I saw it, of course jokingly, as an immaculate conception," she explained.

"So, you were actually insulting me by portraying me as a God-like figure in my own mind?"

"Pretty much, yes. I never considered you God-like to me but rather that *you* felt like you're God, sent here to change the world. Come on, Joel, admit you have an ego."

This was my comeuppance for calling her a diva. What goes around comes around.

"Maybe I do believe that you are here to save the world. I'm deluded about you too," she said, hitting me with a compliment and an insult simultaneously.

While she was on the insult train, she threw another in for good measure.

"Sometimes you sound too much like the tall guy from MSNBC who was lying all the time," she offered up unsolicited.

"Who?"

"The liar."

"Brian Williams?"

"Yes."

"He's not tall. He's my height, like five foot ten. So, you're telling me I sound like an anchor?"

"You need to hear these things from me."

I shook my head and regained control of the conversation.

"Was there anything else about it that you took from our title *Surviving the Survivor*?" I wondered.

"No. I know I can be a tough pain in the ass, so surviving me is an achievement in itself."

"Remember J. L. Cauvin?" I asked.

"Of course, the stand-up comedian."

J. L. does the best Donald Trump impersonation in the country hands down and is a phenomenal stand-up comic. He used to come on the show in the early days as Donald Trump, and we'd roll on the ground from laughter.

"Remember he asked us if we planned to rebrand the podcast once you're dead to '*I Survived the Survivor*?'"

I told J. L. I was going to get T-shirts printed that read, "I *Survived the Survivor* and All I Got Was This Crappy T-shirt." We both laughed thinking about the absurdity of how our now somewhat respectable show began.

"By the way, I have bad news for you."

"What?" My mom scared me a little with her tone.

"I just got back from my annual checkup about half an hour ago. The doctor called me into his office and told me he reviewed all my blood panels. He went to Columbia…"

Like I mentioned earlier, Jewish mothers, mine included, evidently can't use the word "doctor" without attaching both the descriptor "the best" and their university pedigree to it. My mom still sounded serious though, as she continued.

"He's the best internist in Miami Beach. He looked at me with a very solemn voice and said, 'Unless you have an unexpected accident, like you fall and fracture your hip, you'll be here for a while,' he says. 'You are healthy on every level, including mentally.'"

"Mentally, I'm not so sure about," I pushed back.

"I asked the doctor if he thinks the podcast is helping me, and without hesitating, he tells me, 'Yes!'"

"So, I'm basically saving your life, Mom."

"You're saving my brain."

I suppose all people are concerned about their health. But Jewish people, from personal experience, seem to be hyper-focused on what ails them. It made me wonder why— and for a while, it made for one of my favorite *Surviving the Survivor* segments.

"'This Week in Death and Dying' was my brainchild, Mom. We obviously lost it when we pivoted to true crime all the time, but do you miss it?" I asked, chuckling.

"It was funny until it wasn't funny. Like when my own husband made the list. He still hasn't recovered from his double pneumonia and maybe never will."

"I don't get it. Where does all this stem from? You must admit that in Jewish circles we always get a rundown of the 'sick and dying list.' But why?"

I could tell my mom was lost in thought, thinking about my dad and his not-so-slowly declining health. It plagued her worse than his pneumonia did him.

"It is kind of sad that people in this building are dying off in droves. They're too busy dying to enjoy the so-called 'golden years.' You think you're going to be able to enjoy the fruits of your labor, but too many are either sick or dying or both," she concluded.

"You're like an Ordnance Disposal Specialist in Vietnam. It's sort of just a matter of time until you take the wrong step," I added to cheer her up.

"The sad truth is if it's not you or your close family, you say, 'Oh, so sorry.' And you think, *Oh, I am so lucky I escaped!*"

Out of nowhere my mom began asking me a series of unrelated rapid-fire questions related to this very book you're reading right now.

"When is your manuscript due? Are you writing enough each day? Are you trying to make it perfect? You know it has no chance of being a bestseller, right? So, don't make it perfect, just get it done. And, oh yeah, will the publishing company help you market the finished product?"

The flurry of questions irritated me so much I could feel my jaw clenching and my toes curling into tight balls in each shoe.

"Don't unleash your own anxiety on me!" I shouted at her.

"I just asked you something. You are not all there. It's very unfortunate. It's a sad fact that you're not all there."

"I'm stressed out enough about writing. I told you my biggest fear is analysis paralysis and not being able to finish it, and you're asking me if I'm marketing something that's not close to being marketable yet! Why?"

"You need a checkup from the neck up," my mom said, stealing a line from Steve Cohen, who books the best guests in true crime. "I'm just very happy that you spoke with the publisher. I know that authors go on book-signing tours to promote their books, and I was simply asking you if you plan to do the same?" she explained, as I jotted notes down on a napkin so I wouldn't forget what I was going to ask before being distracted by her barrage of non sequiturs.

"Why don't you write on a piece of paper instead of a napkin?"

I had to consciously tell my brain to uncurl my toes and relax my mouth. My mom is the only one who can instantly transform me from a well-adjusted, stable human being into an erratic mess of a man capable of going postal. I had to breathe it out.

"I don't need a piece of paper," I responded calmly with a forced smile. "This napkin is fine. Also, why don't you try to not micromanage my every move for once?"

"What? What?"

The double "whats" were back. We were suddenly and quickly escalating toward war. But I needed this interview done today, and I couldn't afford an explosion of emotion, so I decided on a détente by deftly switching the subject.

"I had another dream that my wife cheated on me, this time with three men."

"Is she a trapeze artist? I hope she cheats on you! What's the big deal? It's just sex!"

"Why do you think I have these recurring dreams that she's cheating on me?"

"Because you're addicted to stress. I just read an article about it, and addiction to stress is real."

Since I was seven, my mom's been quoting all sorts of real and imaginary publications to back up her claims du jour.

"If you can't work yourself up about this book, you'll work yourself up about your wife. You'll always find something to be stressed about until you decide to give up your addiction. It's like smoking or drinking. You need to want to quit yourself."

"By the way, I asked my wife to cut down her massive monthly credit card bill this month. You'll be happy to know she brought it down three hundred dollars," I said sarcastically, as she barely made a dent in the total.

"And what did I tell you?"

"It was a five-digit credit card bill."

"But what did I say to you?"

"You told me she could have gone up five thousand."

"Exactly."

"So, you see a three-hundred-dollar reduction on a ten-thousand-dollar bill as improvement?"

"One hundred percent. Anything that goes down in this case is an improvement."

I was reminded of my mom's unfettered optimism as I began to perseverate about my wife's out-of-control spending going on right before my eyes. I steered the conversation back to our podcast. Was it possible for us to ever stay on track for the duration of an interview? It was a rhetorical question.

"Remember our segment 'Three Questions for Grandma'? Did you enjoy that?" I asked.

"I enjoyed it much more than 'This Week in Dead and Dying' because your kids are smart and asked very intelligent questions for being three, six, and seven. Why did we stop? Oh yeah, because we're doing true crime now," she asked, answering her own question.

"Do you remember a specific question that stood out to you?"

"They asked how God could be everywhere all at once, which I had no idea how to answer. They also asked how babies are made, which I vaguely remember how that's done!"

My mom began scrolling through her phone, which made my toes begin to curl in frustration again.

"Try not to look at your phone while I'm asking questions. I know your time is so valuable," I added condescendingly.

"Who is the control freak now? For you, I'll turn it off. But I'm not like you. I don't get hypnotized."

"Before we switched to true crime, who was your favorite guest?" I asked, redirecting the agitation engendered by my mom's persistent verbal pokes.

"First of all, before I get into that, I have to say something," my mom began, triggering an already accelerated heart rate. I often thought about connecting myself to an iPhone-enabled EKG to see, in real time, how my mother's voice truly impacted my physiology.

"You know I use a lot of curse words when I'm frustrated," she offered up. The only more obvious statement would be if she told me she needed oxygen to survive. She continued, "I don't know if you noticed that lately I use less. Did you notice that?"

"Not really," I answered with incredulity.

The truth is I didn't even really hear my mother's cursing anymore because I had become so immune to it over the years. It would be like asking a transplant surgeon if blood makes them squeamish.

"Well, I'm less frustrated, so I'm cursing less," she revealed proudly like my nine-year-old daughter telling me she got a 100 percent on her spelling test.

"Why don't you curse on the podcast? I mean until now, according to even you, you had previously cursed just about every day of your life, at least since I've known you. So, why not on the show?"

"Because I'm very paranoid by nature, and they say whatever is on YouTube or Spotify or Apple Podcasts lasts forever. So, if I curse, it's forever, and I am not going to expose myself to that."

"But you've cursed during all these sessions. I'm putting it in the book," I explained.

She looked down at my phone then back at me. I waved it in front of her. What a powerful instrument my iPhone had become.

"What, what? When did I curse?" she genuinely asked. The truth is she doesn't even hear her own cursing anymore.

She tried to grab my phone, but, again, my reflexes are no match for hers.

"I will have to take you to a lawyer if you accuse me unjustly."

"There's nothing unjust about it. It's all inside this little computer in my hand."

"Don't do that."

"Don't do what?"

"Don't sell me down the river just to sell a book. Don't throw me under the bus. It's so not right," she pleaded using every cliché in the book, which she surprisingly got right.

It was time to switch gears again.

"We had Carole Baskin on at the height of *Tiger King*. But you'd never heard of the show? How? At the time it was the most watched show ever on Netflix." I was still dumbfounded.

"No, you're right I had never heard of *Tiger King* until Carole Baskin was on. But I haven't heard of many things. I'm usually busy with more important things, and I've just never been that tuned in to the popular culture and dumb TV programs," my mom explained while inadvertently insulting the roughly hundred-plus million people who watched the program.

"You watch TV every night!" I countered.

"Yes, but not the garbage of the garbage. Only the pure garbage that I enjoy," she clarified.

"What did you think of the comparison Carole Baskin made? That you're endangered like her beloved tigers?"

"There is a lot of truth in it."

My mom was now diligently bending a straw and pushing it down into a bottle of vitaminwater, mystifying me in the process.

"Can I ask you why you put your straw back into the bottle? Like, why don't you just leave the straw out? Why jam it in there?" I was genuinely curious.

"Because, um, then I cannot close it. I fold the straw and put it inside the bottle for one simple reason: so I can close it. Is this a problem?"

"Okay, no. No, it isn't." I still didn't really get it.

"It may be weird to you, but there is always a method to my madness."

The mention of Carole Baskin dredged up a joke. My mom is a master of destroying punchlines.

"I heard this very good joke," she began with the obligatory introduction, lest you thought you were about to be told a bad joke. "Jews are so anxious of becoming extinct. This man went to his rabbi and told him, 'I'm terrified our people will be lost and gone soon, so I must have as many children as possible,' she continued. "The rabbi tells the young man to calm down and relax. The man is confused and then the rabbi tells him to take a cue from my son. 'Your son?' the man asks. 'Yes, my son. He's gay. They don't even procreate and they're everywhere!'"

I told my mom some might find the joke offensive, and she asked me not to include it. I told her it's my obligation to present an accurate portrayal of her. She unsuccessfully tried to grab my phone again.

"Who was another favorite pre–true crime guest?" I asked.

"Dara Horn," she answered with zero hesitation.

"Why?"

"Well, she wrote, *People Love Dead Jews*. I thought it was a very smart book."

"What was the premise of the book in a nutshell?"

"Exactly what the title says. The world loves Jews but prefers dead ones. Poland, for example, has big celebrations every year with concerts to memorialize the three and a half million Jews murdered during the war. But barely any Jews still live there, yet they make a big deal out of it. At the Anne Frank museum in Amsterdam, one of the tour guides was asked to remove his yarmulke at work. It's a memorial to a Jewish heroine, but they wanted its employee to hide his Judaism. This is the insanity of our world, and Dara Horn hit the proverbial nail on the head in *People Love Dead Jews*."

She stopped suddenly and motioned with her hand like she was done speaking.

"Who cares about this?" she said. "Let's not talk about this. It's a boring subject. Let's talk about something else."

So I continued with the Jewish theme, of course.

"We had on the daughter of a Holocaust survivor and the grandson of a Nazi, and it didn't go quite as planned," I reminded my mom.

"They were doing a speaking tour together in England," my mom recalled quickly.

"I was sure you were going to go after the Nazi's grandson, but you threw me off when you eviscerated that poor woman, the Holocaust survivor's child."

"They both saw my true colors. I really ripped into her."

"What got you so mad about them and especially her?" I wanted to know. When I booked that episode, I knew it would be explosive. But it was worse than I thought.

"There should be more love and kindness. There should be more kindness in the world." My mom mimicked the woman's grief-stricken tone. "Implying if there was more love and kindness in the world maybe the Nazis wouldn't have murdered six million Jews. What a fucking Pollyanna she was with her head in the clouds. She really pissed me off. And then they told me how it helps *them* to go to synagogues and give speeches. Like it's all about *them*!" My mom was now fully reliving this unhinged interview. "Who the hell needs them to go to synagogues and give speeches? They need to speak out against anti-Semitism in Europe, which is rampant now. The Christians should be speaking up, not the Jews!"

Maybe my mom was right just a few minutes ago when she suggested we move off the Jewish-themed topics. It was probably best for her health. Certain things really riled her up, and this was one of them.

"I cannot stand these pie-in-the-sky people! They were speaking to Holocaust survivors! For what? To tell them about all the atrocities that they lived through. She said some survivors hugged her at the end. They should've slapped her."

It was definitely time to move away from discussing Jews, but this was easier said than done I quickly found out.

"What did you think of Dr. Avi Loeb?" I asked, speaking of the famous Harvard astrophysicist whom we had on too. He has a bestselling book called *Extraterrestrial* about discovering what he believes was an alien spaceship deep in the universe.

"You want to know the truth?" My mom would frequently begin sentences with this question as a way to prepare me for an unexpected answer. "He bored me!"

We laughed because one thing you can't say about Dr. Loeb is that he's boring. He's super smart and very charismatic and even told us some major movie studios optioned his story as an Israeli citizen becoming an outspoken American scholar.

"He's a smart Jewish boy," my mom finally relented about the sixty-one-year-old astrophysicist. "One day, we'll probably all have to tell him he was right about the spaceship."

"Ben Ferencz was another very interesting character," my mom continued unsolicited.

It was clear my mom loved some dead Jews too. Ben Ferencz, who passed away just last year at 103, was the last surviving prosecutor from the Nuremberg trials. Interestingly, it was the first case he ever tried and arguably the biggest courtroom case of all time.

"What was his famous slogan?" my mom asked, unable to recall it herself.

"Law not war," I reminded her.

"Oh yeah."

"You called him a Pollyanna too," I reminded her.

"Well, unfortunately, sadly, I wish he were right and not me. Everyone works to make this world a perfect, little idyllic place. But the truth is it's very messy, ugly, and a uniquely cruel place, and that means the rule of law, in reality, usually is incapable of keeping people from war. Ukraine is a perfect example. Remember we had that couple on live from Kyiv at the very beginning of the war?"

"I do remember that very well."

I had found a couple that livestreamed with us as bombs landed on the outskirts of Kyiv. They were trapped in a laundry room with their two cats.

"Write that down so you can add it," my mom strongly suggested.

"I'm not writing down anything because I have this cell phone, which also happens to be capturing your every word, including the bad ones," I told her.

She had some choice words for the Ukrainians at the beginning of the war. I wanted to get her on the record, so to speak, but I knew she'd be too paranoid to repeat what she had once told me. I tried though.

"Is it still your opinion that the Ukrainians were not very helpful to the Jews during World War Two?" I asked, knowing she had called them notorious anti-Semites.

"They were just like everybody else except the righteous Gentiles who helped the Jews," she answered politically, knowing my cell phone wouldn't lie.

"So, how do you explain to everyone how and why we eventually settled on true crime as our niche?" I asked.

"Well, you just said it. We were advised by many people to find a niche. Before true crime, we were dabbling in all sorts of stories, but our audience didn't know what we were really all about. We learned quickly that no one really cares about me or you but instead about the subjects we cover."

My mom's right about this. Along the way, I reunited with a friend from my Fox News days who specialized in booking network guests. Steve Cohen, whom I've mentioned earlier, became an integral part of our team. He's the Sandy Koufax of guest bookers. My wife is fondly and accurately known as the COE, which stands for Chief Of Everything, and SpacedCoast is my brother-in-law, so it's really a family affair, along with our amazing mods who keep our chats civil.

"Without our team we'd be nothing. We met Steve Cohen through pure serendipity," my mom added. "He's a fun person, and a news junkie, and he got fixated on a true crime story that was connected to us right here in south Florida."

Dan Markel's story was featured on *Dateline*, *20/20*, and the Wondery podcast network. He was a Canadian who went to Harvard undergrad and law school and was a prominent legal scholar teaching at Florida State University. He was tragically shot and killed in his Tallahassee driveway back in 2014. Authorities discovered two hitmen were responsible for Dan's murder. They were eventually convicted along with an intermediary. Just last year, Dan's ex-brother-in-law Charlie Adelson was indicted for the heinous crime. Soon after, the Adelson matriarch, Donna, was arrested too and charged with murder.

"Once we got into Dan Markel's case, we looked at our numbers, and they were like, really good," my mom recounted. "And we really got into it. And it was a Jewish story."

Why couldn't we avoid all things Jewish? Maybe it was *bashert*, a Yiddish word meaning "meant to be."

"It was sort of about us in an odd way. Donna Adelson was this overbearing Jewish mother, ahem, ahem"—my mom cleared her throat for dramatic effect—"who was probably too close to her children, especially her son Charlie. And it also had a big psychological appeal, which we both really enjoy."

We found our niche and developed an amazing community we affectionately refer to as "STS Nation," who have been on this magical ride ever since. We went from doing one show a week to every day but Saturday. To paraphrase a line from *The Big Lebowski*, "We sure as shit don't roll on Shabbos!" My mom still hosts one day a week. And we are always live, which allows STS Nation to chat in real time from all corners of the world.

"In your wildest dreams when I pitched this, did you ever think that we would have over one hundred thousand people following us? Our growth happened very quickly and doesn't seem to be stopping anytime soon."

"This makes me think of the Woody Allen joke," my mom said as I waited for her to screw it up. " He says he took a summer course in music, which began with 'Yankee Doodle' and progressed to Beethoven's Fifth and back to 'Yankee Doodle.' I'm afraid we'll go from Beethoven's Fifth, which is our one hundred thousand followers, back to 'Yankee Doodle,' which is like, going back to our two thousand subscribers."

My mom doesn't handle success well. It simply makes her too nervous, and now our relative success gave her pause for concern that it could all vanish in an instant. I tried to make her even more uncomfortable.

"There are some months that we've had more than two million views."

"I can't even, I can't even, I can't fathom that number. I mean, that's unbelievable. And the one interesting thing that is still the most interesting is that it's the whole globe."

She then found an opening to take my baseline anxiety level from a nine to a ten.

"Joel, if you do it earlier in the day, I think we'll get even more viewers overseas."

Whenever I was somewhat comfortable and relaxed, my mom would project her own insecurities on me, which in turn would drive me insane.

"Let me handle the producing and scheduling, Mom. You're just the talent."

She loved that reference.

"Why do you think there's such an insatiable appetite for true crime?" I pushed forward.

"I will tell you why because I'm an expert on most things, but especially this. TV stations are really losing viewers rapidly. Everything in this country changes very fast. True crime has always been a popular niche from Agatha Christie to Dr. Jackal and Mr. Hyde."

"It's Jekyll, not Jackal," I corrected her. "A jackal is an animal native to Africa and Eurasia."

"Jekyll, yeah, whatever. Anyway, true crime has been around since Cain murdered Abel and likely way before that even."

"Do you think people now are more intrigued by the psychology behind true crime?" I asked.

"Yes, it's a challenge, a real mystery to figure it all out. What was the motivation? These are all curious questions that people look for answers to," my mom explained.

"By the way, do you attribute our success to me or you or to the subject matter?" I wanted to know.

"It's obviously all because of me," my mom joked. "I think it's a combination. Fifty percent is the subject matter, twenty-five percent our guests, and twenty-five percent your interviewing skills. By some divine providence, we miraculously found this niche."

The truth is my mom is a huge part of the success. She's still super sharp and, as a licensed therapist, brings unique perspective to each story, along with her wisdom from all she's endured in her eighty-four years. My mom is definitely this cult of personality. People get genuinely upset with me for my perceived, or maybe real, lack of patience when it comes to her getting her points across "on air." She reminds me frequently that English is not her first language and therefore it takes her longer to process her thoughts. She still needs to spit out her questions faster. I run a tight ship.

"I just got a—a hate letter from a woman in Germany of all places," I shared with my mom. "She's accusing me of hating my mother. I wanted to write back, 'Fuck you and everyone you know for gassing my grandfather,' but then I realized this was probably not the best approach."

"Why do you care what she says? She's dead to us," my mom chimed in. It wasn't that she was German. My mom is fiercely loyal, and anyone who snipes at her son is nonexistent in her mind. This was no exception.

"May I, may I ask you something?" my mom often prefaces questions with a question announcing she's going to ask a question. "I want an honest answer. Do I change into somebody who I am not, into some persona, during the show?"

"Yes," I snapped back, not giving her the answer she wanted, explaining, "you don't curse on air. You are much looser with your lips before and after the show."

She looked a touch discouraged and disparaged.

"Do you plan to leave me a little more when you're gone because I put you on the map at eighty-four?" I joked, asking about a modest inheritance currently reserved down the middle for my sister, Arden, and me.

"One hundred percent no!" she exclaimed.

"What about the fact that I gave you a little taste of celebrity in your golden years? It's worth nothing to you?"

"No, it's worth nothing to you because you're not getting a penny more. You're sick. Who would even think about this?"

I can't say this news wasn't disappointing. I'm sure my sister will be happy to read this now, though.

"Is it fun for you?" I asked.

"It's one hundred percent fun. It's some of the best times I've had in this stage of life."

My mom has received letters and emails from all around the world simply thanking her for still being alive and well enough to host a show.

"I have to tell you, Joel, I get such an outpouring of positive comments. Very few people say, 'Get that old woman out of there. She serves no purpose,'" my mom said proudly.

"Actually, more than a few people have said something along those lines," I joked. "Why do you check your show numbers and listen to every episode as soon as it's over? I hate watching myself," I explain.

"Because if I don't love myself, who will?"

Then my mom got somewhat serious, at least for this moment.

"Listen, I'm not under the illusion that this little show immortalized me. But it certainly made me be taken more seriously while I'm here. I'm not just forgotten in an old age home or assisted-living facility. I am living in the world with you and everyone else. So many people my age are just discarded by society."

My dad was currently one of these exiled elderly Americans.

"Does it keep your mind sharp?"

"Yes, it keeps my mind sharp. And, you see, I'm not embarrassed if I have a senior moment. I say it right on the show. I don't know if you noticed."

"Trust me, I've noticed." We both laughed.

"By the way, do we think we will ever run out of true crime?" I asked as my neurosis set back in.

"No, only false crime," my mom quipped.

"Any final thoughts on this podcast?"

"Uh, I was right to give birth to you because even though you are a pain in the ass, I think you give me back so much. Can you imagine if I had only one child? Thank God I had you and Arden. And aren't you so happy with your three beautiful children? And your smart and gorgeous wife? It so happens that I like your wife."

She didn't really answer my question. But I knew she was happy, and that made me happy.

Actual Voicemail from My Mom: *August 7, 2022*

Jo-el,

It's your loving mother.

I cannot get on the Safari, and they say you cannot have the meeting without the Safari because the camera won't work without the Safari.

So, I tried on the computer to get on the meeting. I tried on the phone, which doesn't work. Something else pops up.

[Click]

"I HAVE 178,000 UNOPENED EMAILS"

I was running late for a discussion with my mom about technology. I rolled up to her Miami Beach condo in my Tesla, the lowest no-frills Model 3, just to be clear. It cost less, surprisingly, than our Chrysler Pacifica minivan, which I happened to really love, despite originally declaring I'd never become *that* dad. The Tesla had been driving me crazy lately because the electronics needed updating, causing certain doors not to open. Late, I screeched in hurriedly and handed my key card to the valet. I raced through the lobby only to find an unusually long line of residents waiting at the elevator banks because two were out of service. Was God sending me a not-so-subtle message about technology, I wondered. After an uncharacteristically long twenty-minute wait, I finally made it up to the twenty-seventh floor.

My mom answered the door. "Didn't I tell you I had things to do today?"

"I'm sorry I'm writing your memoir, Mom."

"How many times have I told you? You're writing this book for you, not me. You think it'll help our podcast. You want to be an author. The book should be called *Ten Percent Karmela,*

Ninety Percent Joel: A Memoir about My Mom," she strongly suggested.

"My Tesla is all out of whack. Your building's elevators aren't working. Maybe we're better off living with the technological accoutrements of 1939 Subotica, Yugoslavia. What tech did you have back then, anyway?" I dove right into our conversation to avoid further criticism from my beloved mother.

"We had a very beautiful radio. There was generally one radio per family, and that was it!" she exclaimed, almost proudly.

"That's so crazy compared to what we have now," I stated the obvious, unable to begin to imagine life with just a radio. Wow.

"And, as far as transportation..." my mom continued, but there was a knock at the door. It aggravated the crap out of me because these interview sessions with my mom were sacred. It was our time to buckle down and focus, even though her phone usually buzzed or drills in the building buzzed overhead. But now, there was a knock at the door. I slammed my palms on the table in frustration.

"Relax, Joel!" my mom screamed.

"Who is it?" I asked clearly aggravated.

I swung the door open. It was the valet from downstairs.

"Sorry to bother you," he said, even though it was already too late.

"I gave you the key," I explained. Teslas use a key card, not a traditional car key, which I had intentionally left in the cup holder.

"I know, sir, but it's not working."

"I don't understand why you don't have a regular key," my mom chimed in from the dining room table, agitating me even further.

"Did you try swiping it correctly?" I asked the valet, who looked at me like an idiot, having parked an innumerable number of Teslas.

"Joel, go down with him and help him move it!" my mom barked orders from just around the corner.

"It just took me twenty minutes to get up here because your elevators are down, and now you want me to go down and come back up? That'll be forty minutes!" I snapped.

Poor valet man was now collateral damage in the battle between my mom and me.

"There's no way in hell I'm going back down!"

"It's your fault for buying a fancy car that's basically a computer on wheels," my mom said, raising her voice.

"It's called technology, Mom." I was ready to explode. "It's what I'd be discussing with you right now, if not for all these problems." I was so irritated because I had to take off soon to pick my kids up from school.

"He's waiting," my mom said, attempting to guilt me into helping him.

He was watching us like he was a spectator at a tennis match at the Miami Open.

"Maybe use your phone to open the car?" the valet offered in broken English.

Teslas use an app system whereby you can unlock the car remotely using just your phone.

"I go down and you open," he suggested.

What a great idea. In the heat of the moment, I forgot I could simply unlock my car and he'd be able to drive it into the garage.

"I call you," the valet said as he retreated down the elevators.

"This is why technology makes me so nervous and stressed out." My mom used the moment to offer her blanket opinion on tech.

My toes were cramping because I was now rolling them into such a tight ball in my shoes.

My phone rang. The high-pitched ring tone triggered instant heart palpitations. I answered as fast as I could.

"It's Jean Pierre," the valet announced himself by name.

I already had the app open and unlocked the car. Jean Pierre was able to get in my car and move it to a safe spot. *Maybe technology isn't so bad after all,* I thought. My mom remained unimpressed.

"I don't understand why everything is so complicated now," she said, as she scrolled through Instagram on her phone.

"Put your phone down. Immediately," I said.

"Fuck off! Don't tell me what to do," my mom pushed back.

Everything was back to normal, at least for the moment. And we continued our discussion, ironically, about the incredible advancement of technology during her lifetime.

"So, you had a radio," I picked back up, "Where was the radio in your house? What did it look like? How big was it? What did you listen to on it?"

"The radio was the size of, uh, well, I'm trying to see what I can compare it to." She began to stand to look around her condo for something comparable.

"I don't need to see anything," I explained. "Was it bigger than a toaster oven and smaller than a fridge?" I asked.

"It was closer to a toaster than a fridge, probably about two by two feet," she gesticulated, outlining the shape with her hands. "It had a beautiful exterior like a piece of antique furniture, but it had a lot of static," she explained.

"What would you listen to?" I asked curiously.

"My stepfather listened to classical music. But the truth is we didn't even use it that much. During my college years in Switzerland, my aunt Anne Laure and I would listen to the radio all the time. They still didn't have a television in the late 1950s, so we regularly listened to radio dramas and plays."

I surveyed my mom's apartment quickly. There was a digital thermostat, a smart TV, and an even smarter refrigerator. How could so much have changed in one woman's lifetime? It was really hard to fathom how her world transformed so radically so relatively quickly.

"There was nothing, to this day, that I enjoyed more than listening to those plays on the radio. It leaves everything to your fantasy. The beautiful woman is exactly the way you imagine her. The gangster is just as tough as you expect him to be."

The weird thing is I still listen to the radio myself for many of the same reasons. There was a legendary radio host named Art Bell who had a show called *Coast to Coast AM* about all sorts of far-out things like aliens, UFOs, conspiracy theories, and stories about Bigfoot and Chupacabras. It still exists, and I still love listening to it late at night, and I wonder if subconsciously it has to do with my own mom's love for the medium.

"My stepfather was also an amazing pianist. We used to sit in our living room in Subotica mesmerized by his playing," she added.

All I could think was if I grew up listening to my dad playing piano, I'd probably be institutionalized from boredom. I don't know how my mom's generation survived, to be honest. No TVs. No cell phones. No laptops. No X, formerly Twitter. How? Well, X I could certainly do without I'll openly concede.

I'd been hacked out of Facebook a few months back and didn't miss it a lick.

"Reading was also a really popular form of entertainment."

I was still hung up on no television during her college years. "Wait, so your entire university career you had no television at all?"

"What don't you get? Absolutely not. Nobody in that part of Europe had televisions, even in the early sixties."

I felt anxiety wondering how I'd fill so much of my time if I didn't have a television to waste it on. While I was growing up, my mom would call me a "hollow head" whenever she thought I was watching too much TV.

"We were just lucky to have electricity and indoor plumbing and toilets." My mom became more animated. "A lot of the neighboring towns only had kerosene lamps and outhouses. You know, like a big hole in the ground with a wooden seat, if you were lucky. And it was cold as hell outside."

"And in what was then Yugoslavia, you had no cars either, right?" I asked.

"What cars? There were zero cars. Zero. Do you understand the word 'zero'?" she asked rhetorically. "Whenever we needed to go somewhere, we'd have to book a horse and buggy the day beforehand. Just like in Central Park today, we only had horse and buggy with a little chariot in the back. My father would walk to city hall, where you'd make a reservation for wherever you needed to go."

My mom explained that all of Subotica was just a square mile or so. But if you needed to get to the train station, you'd need to order the horse ahead of time.

How would Domino's pizza delivery work back then? I wondered, "Did you have to pay these horse and buggy drivers?"

"Of course, it was like a taxi," my mom answered incredulously. "Everything you needed, everything you wanted, like the post office, the school, the stores, everything was within a one-and-a-half-mile radius."

"When was the first time you remember ever seeing a television set?"

"My uncle's house," she answered.

"Please don't give me one-word answers," I warned her for the umpteenth time.

"It was actually three," my mom said, then added, "Don't be a little bitch."

"Well, this is supposed to be a book, not a blog post," I said.

"What is a blog, exactly?" my mom asked.

"I have no idea," I confessed. "It's a modern-day word for an article."

"I probably saw a television for the first time at my uncle's apartment in Switzerland in the mid-1960s."

"And do you remember your first thought when you saw it?"

"Yes, I do. This is a fabulous technology. Fabulous. I liked it," my mom said with a wide-eyed smile.

"Now that you see how far technology has advanced, do you feel like your childhood was stripped of so much because none of this was available to you?" I wanted to know. "I mean, you love television, Mom. You're hypnotized by it."

"Honestly, we didn't know there was another option. I was lucky because, unlike you, I read. Reading makes you smart, and TV generally makes you dumb!" she said staring intently at me. "We also had three beautiful movie houses. I watched all the classics like *Gone with the Wind* and so many incredible European films."

"How often would you go to the movies?"

"They changed every week. And I went as often as I could. I loved to get lost in a great movie, especially after the harsh reality of World War Two. It was nice to be able to lose yourself in a great story. I'd see Italian, French, American, and Russian films."

"Were there ratings like PG or R?"

"No, definitely not. I saw more nudity and more sex in those early years than ever since. And no one thought twice about it. I watched an Italian film called *The Lovers of Verona*, and my eyes were popping out of my head. It was a twist on Romeo and Juliet, and it was basically porn."

"Speaking of porn and technology," I segued, "did you see that article I sent you today on OnlyFans?" I asked.

"What? What is OnlyFans?" she asked, confused.

"It's a website where predominantly women make a shit ton of money, usually shedding a lot of clothing in the process," I explained as she rolled her eyes. "You can roll your eyes all you want, but some of these 'creators' are making more than four hundred thousand dollars a month."

"Here we go again with your money obsession. You know something is wrong with you. I mean it, something isn't wired right in your brain," my mom exclaimed. "Why don't you create a vagina and breasts and get on...what's it called again?"

"It's OnlyFans. Would you become a creator, Mom? There are men out there with weird fetishes for, let me put it this way, mature women," I said. "It'd be a hell of a lot more money than we're making with our podcast right now."

"Yes, I'd start the eighty-four and more category! But gravity is not my friend these days."

"Do it for me. I could really use four hundred thousand a month."

"Something's really, really wrong with you."

I shifted the conversation back on course, even though this was a disturbingly fun rabbit hole we had momentarily descended into.

"Your generation has probably seen the biggest shift in technology. I mean, you literally went from the railroad and the Industrial Revolution to virtual reality and artificial intelligence."

"I mean I never even flew in a plane until I was married. We flew from London to Paris just to see what it feels like to fly."

"What a crazy thought. Did you like the experience?"

"I hid it all from my mother because she was deathly afraid of flying and couldn't wrap her head around how something so big could float through the sky. And I hated every second of it. I have a fear of flying because of my mother, not because of Erica Jong!"

"Which piece of technology have you marveled at the most in your lifetime?" I asked curiously.

"This." She pointed to her cell phone. "Remember how much phone calls used to cost? It was a fortune. I always had family in Europe and just speaking to them almost bankrupted me. Now, I can speak for hours, which I do, and it's a flat rate."

"You wonder where I get my money anxiety from?" I glared at my mom. "I oddly remember thinking the overseas operator worked in a booth in the middle of the Atlantic Ocean, equidistant to America and Europe, sort of like the toll-takers on the New Jersey Turnpike."

"It would be an underseas operator, not overseas" is all my mom had to add.

"And now you talk to your sister in Hungary every day, and it costs you nothing."

"Not true. It costs me a lot of nerves."

"So, you just talked about the cost, but I'm asking you, what piece of technology would you say is the most amazing or remarkable to you?"

"It's not only the cost. This cell phone is a computer in your hand. When I first saw a computer, it literally filled an entire room. They only existed in the corporate world. Now, everyone has a minicomputer right in the palm of their hand. If that's not remarkable I don't know what is."

"What's it like for you to deal with the ever-evolving landscape of technology? Is it hard for you to keep up on the latest trends? For example, you *claim* to have never heard of OnlyFans."

"It's difficult. But not because of the technology per se. It's because of the type of person I am. I just don't have the patience to learn everything, and, quite frankly, I don't care that much either. Technology requires one to be so precise."

"Try to answer my questions, please."

"I just did, but maybe you were daydreaming of someone on OnlyFans."

"Well, then elaborate a little bit. I'd hate to force you to offer your perspective for *your book* about *you.*"

"Everything in technology must be precise. In other words, if I'm sending an email, I must make sure I have the period in the right spot, or it won't send it. You have to have that point between the first and last name, for example."

"It's called a 'dot.' That's *why* it's dot-com and not peri-od-com or point-com," I said with joy visible in every crevice of my face.

"I meant to say dot. I just don't have the patience for it all. I am very people oriented. I'm not into this mechanical, impersonal, cold relationship, which you evidently have with your internet!"

"I had to take a computer language called Pascal in high school, and I had to cheat off Steve Isakoff the entire year. Pascal, as far as I know, doesn't even exist anymore. But my now four-year-old son, Judah Mac, can already understand and use everything. He knows how to do certain things that I don't even know how to do. A lot of things, in fact."

"Listen, even your dog knows how to open doors. Even dogs have changed," my mom joked, although it's true that my boxer Ethel Bug can open a door with her unusually dexterous paw.

"What do you think of your grandchildren, that at the age of five, eight, and ten are already tech masters? They call them digital natives, you know."

"I didn't know that reference, but it makes sense. Digital natives!"

"What do you think of them?"

"Well, I think that they're fast. They are not afraid that they will make a mistake that will erase things. They don't even think about that possibility, which the older adults do. It's funny because I remember as if it were today when the internet was in its infancy. I had a client, and she told me how easy it was to use. She said, 'You just have to punch in this number and punch in that number and punch in there!' And I swear I said to her, 'I'll wait until we can just talk to the computer, and the computer will follow.' And now you can talk to the computer, and the computer will follow your instructions. Now I really have no excuses!"

"When online banking first started, did it make you nervous that people would steal your money?"

"No, but I'll tell you what I was very nervous about. The microwave oven was terrifying to me because we weren't sure if you could be radiated from it."

This one comment validated so much for me about my life and childhood. I wasn't born an anxious, neurotic Jew. I was groomed into one.

"So did you stay away from microwaves?" I needed to know. Understanding the entire fabric of my being depended on her answer.

"Well, luckily for us, Arno Penzias was our neighbor. For those who don't know him, he won the Nobel Prize in Physics for the big bang theory…"

"It's a great show!" I interrupted.

"What? What?"

"Never mind." It went right over my mom's head as I suspected it would.

"Anyway, Arno always carried a radiation gauge with him, and he would check to make sure the microwave wasn't leaking, which gave me great peace of mind."

"And this is normal?"

"Maybe it leaked a little bit, and that's why you are the way you are," my mom jabbed back.

"You used to yell at me because I'd hold the cell phone up to my ear."

"Well, just like the microwave, I read or heard somewhere that it can cause a brain tumor. Looking at you now, maybe it only affected you slightly." My mom was on a roll.

"Does technology overwhelm you?"

"In general, I am not afraid of the internet or technology. But I'll tell you what does overwhelm me. I have one hundred and seventy-eight thousand unopened emails on my iPhone."

"That you haven't opened?" I was confused as this was new to me.

"Um, yes that I opened but never erased."

"It's deleted. The word is 'deleted.' Why haven't you deleted one hundred and seventy-eight thousand emails?"

"I just can't keep up. There is so much advertising and so much irrelevant stuff. The spam is something else. By the way, none of the one hundred and seventy-eight thousand are spam."

I was stunned she knew what spam was and was even using it correctly in a sentence.

"So, you have one hundred and seventy-eight thousand emails from people you know, and you've just chosen not to delete them. Why?"

"I have no idea. But I thought for sure one day my phone would explode. But so far it didn't."

"Do you have trouble understanding the notion of a cloud? That all your data goes into a cloud?" It's something I couldn't wrap my head around either.

"No, I have no trouble understanding this," my mom answered surprisingly. "It's like a warehouse. That's how I visualize it. Like an Amazon warehouse filled with information instead of soap and shampoo."

"You don't picture a cloud?" I asked incredulously.

"No, I don't," she answered nonchalantly.

"Does it make you nervous, though, that all your information is out there?"

"No, it just confirms my paranoia. And I feel justified that I was right about..."

"About what?"

"About the fact that Big Brother knows everything. I was looking for a dress for my granddaughter's wedding, and I went on one of the sites. Now I'm flooded with advertisements for gowns, and the deluge won't stop. Amazon reminds me I'm almost out of my hand cream. Big Brother knows everything and then some!"

"They say phones can hear you now," I said, trying to add to her paranoia.

"Well, I know that they can hear me."

"Does it make you nervous?"

"Very honestly, very honestly. You want to know the absolute truth? Yes, it does make me nervous. It's like an invasion of my life. They think they know everything about me. That's what annoys me."

"They don't *think* they know everything. They *do* know everything," I clarified.

My mom got up and looked around her apartment to emphasize that she felt like she was being spied on. She also had to pee, which put me out another twenty minutes. Everything takes her so much longer to do now, and it's why my kids have affectionately nicknamed her "the Sloth."

"If Jeff Bezos came up to you in the mid-nineties and told you he wanted to start an online bookstore, would you have invested?" I asked.

"Remember what a nerd he was?" she answered. "Now he has muscles and a young woman. The bastard divorced his wife."

"Stick to answering my questions. Pretend this is a deposition. Would you have invested?"

"Absolutely not. I'm not a risk-taker. One of our friend's sons went to work for Amazon. Wait, are you recording?" she stopped suddenly and asked.

"Yes, I'm recording everything."

"Well, then never mind, it's none of your business! It's off the record!"

"Just tell me whatever you were going to say. It's just between us and the three people who are going to read this!"

"Fuck off, Joel."

"Whatever, I'm too tired to beg you to speak for your own book. Back to my question about Bezos. If he ran the Amazon idea by you in 1995, would you have invested?"

"I would've told him to fuck off too and turned him down immediately. Hands down!"

"Besides *fuck off*, what would you have said to him?"

"I would have said, 'Sorry, I don't want to do this right now. I have a family. We have a house. It's too much risk,'" she explained.

"You couldn't imagine people would buy books online?"

"Listen, I've had offers over the years to invest in various things, and I've almost always turned them down. And, in just about every case, I was right. In the Jeff Bezos case, I would've been incredibly wrong, and that's why I'm not wealthy like him. All these very successful businesspeople all have one common denominator: they are all risk-takers."

"Back to online banking for a moment. Does it make you nervous to execute transactions online?"

"For full disclosure, I still don't bank online!"

"What? You told me you did!"

"I mean, I have an online bank account. But I have no idea how to use it. Arden helps me with it. I can get to my online bank, but your sister sets up all my automatic withdrawals. And I can check it on my phone. But that's it."

"Why wouldn't you just bother to learn how to bank online?"

"If I learn a new thing at my age, and I don't do it all the time, then I tend to forget how to do what I have learned. But I'm very proud when I can do something with this goddamn technology. A lot of times I forget my passcodes. There are so many passwords, and when I can't remember them, I get blocked, and that makes me very agitated. In a lot of ways, life was much easier before technology, now that we're talking about it."

"But technology has also brought you a level of fame, albeit small, in your golden years. Did you ever think you'd find a scintilla of celebrity at eighty-four on, of all things, YouTube?"

"Very honestly, I thought we were going to discuss the podcast."

"What do you think I was just asking you about?" I waved in front of her face. "Are you here? Anyone home?"

"You mentioned celebrity so I got confused," She paused to think. "Well, I thought it was a podcast question, but I will answer it graciously. It's probably the wildest thing to happen to me in my eighty-second, eighty-third, and eighty-fourth years. People cannot believe I have a show on YouTube, and to be honest, I can't believe it either."

"It is strange. I spent twenty-seven years working in broadcast news, a lot of them on air, and in all that time I think I got two dozen emails from viewers, and usually they wrote to tell me they hated my tie. One time, while reporting for Fox 5 in New York City, I said 'porn' shop instead of 'pawn.' That got a heavy response. But, now that we have our podcast, as you know, we get dozens of emails and tweets every day. It is bizarre but a lot of fun."

"Did you say fun?" my mom asked. "I thought you were only capable of misery and suffering. Maybe technology really is transformative."

I ignored her insult. "What's being on YouTube and all these different audio platforms done for you psychologically?"

"Well, psychologically, I am not so sure. But you don't have to believe me; it has really helped me counter aging. It's revolutionary for me in terms of feeling and staying young."

"How so?" I was intrigued.

"Well, contrary to what you think, I work on the shows I co-host with you. I research the topics, I read books, and I google everything I need to know. It keeps my mind sharp in the same way doing crossword puzzles helped me. Now that your dad is in Miami Jewish, I don't really do crosswords anymore. Instead, I just focus on true crime, which I love because it's mostly based in psychology."

My mom loved analyzing crimes while trying to understand what motivated different, unconscionable acts.

"I'm a very modest person. But even I'm impressed with me. How many women my age have the chutzpah to get in front of a camera and microphone and host a show?"

"Don't get too carried away." I reminded her, "I still do most of the work, and you don't touch anything related to the tech side of things!"

"Any stupid technician can do that. But to show up at eighty-four and put in my three cents and carry on like a lunatic for an hour and a half, it's a lot."

"It's two cents, not three. So, you're proud of yourself?"

"I am very proud of that."

"And are you proud of your son who started it all?"

"I'm very grateful to my son."

"Wow, so gracious of you to shower me with such kindness."

"You deserve some. But not too much."

"Okay, I don't have all the time in the world here. So let me throw some numbers at you because I always do my home-work. Facebook has two-point-nine billion users in the world. YouTube has two-point-one billion users. Instagram has one-point-three billion. TikTok has one billion. What do you think about the fact that basically the entire world is hooked on these apps? I mean, three billion people is half the world."

"You know, when they said that, what is the term? Um, what is the term? You know when they say that commerce is now international..." she asked during a senior moment.

"Global?"

"Global. Global. Global, okay," she repeated as to not forget it the next time. "You can see how everything of this nature is global."

"Like when we do our show, there are people watching and listening from all around the world," I said proudly.

"They are from all over, all over, from places you never thought they would be from like Tasmania. It's the same YouTube there, right?" my mom asked quizzically.

"No, they have the secret Tasmanian devil YouTube," I joked. "What do you think about the prevalence of these social media sites?"

We have viewers and listeners from the UK, New Zealand, the Republic of Ireland, India, Canada, Mexico, El Salvador, Brazil, Cameroon, and Israel, just to name a few.

"I think it's wonderful. The world has become so much smaller. And these different companies compete against each other, so that's healthy too, at least from a business perspec-tive," my mom said.

"But there's a dark side to tech too," I told my mom. "A ten-year study at BYU discovered that teenage girls at age thirteen who spent two to three hours daily on social media were at a much higher risk for suicide as young adults. It has also been shown that adolescents who experience cyberbullying had much greater symptoms of depression. Their suicidal ideation is higher too. Researchers say that social media is potentially harmful psychologically because people see, you know, these idyllic photos of other people, and they start to feel more and more isolated. So, what about the negative side of technology, especially for young children? What is your advice?"

"It's so simple, really. Parents need to do their job and really know what their kids are doing. You don't have to be a helicopter parent, but you must know how your children are spending their time. And you need to occasionally ask them how they're feeling. I mean, kids can be watching psychologically damaging things, and I don't just mean porn."

"After a lot of these mass shootings, we find out the shooter was either bullied, cyberbullied, or they were obsessed with video games, or isolated, or all the above. So do you believe there is this dark, sinister side to technology also?"

"Definitely, definitely." My mom was giving this substantial thought. "Throughout history there has always been a dark side to society. I mean, we see this every day in the types of stories we cover on *Surviving the Survivor*. The world is a crazy place, and that, unfortunately, will never change. Has technology made it worse? Probably, yes. Considerably worse because there's such easy access to negative forces, which tempt people with dark proclivities."

"What about cynics who say Facebook, Instagram, TikTok, and YouTube purposefully try to get the user addicted to the technology?"

"Well, you know what your father says all the time."

"What?"

"He says milk is a gateway drug because we all start off drinking it. But it's up to us to make the right choices."

"Now that sounded like the old person with wisdom who I've been looking for. Too bad Dad can't really speak anymore, otherwise I might be writing a book about him instead."

"It'd be a hell of a lot more interesting than anything I have to say," she insisted yet again. "Why don't you rewrite *Humanistic Psychiatry: From Oppression to Choice?*"

"That's my next book. But for now, focus," I reined her in. "What advice do you have to people who are overwhelmed with the onslaught of technology?"

"It's very simple: do what I do. I say my name is Karmela Waldman. I am eighty-four. I am very twentieth century. I wasn't born with a computer under my arm, and I am not good with computers. Please, kindly don't tell me to go on the website. I am still a phone person."

"Well, thanks for that advice, but I meant psychologically, not technically. It overwhelms people. They spend too much time isolated on their devices."

"Again, it's simple: everything in moderation. Just make sure you're mindful and do not do what is too much for you. Each person is different and therefore their tolerance can range so much."

"What advice would you have for your granddaughter if she came to you and said she was feeling depressed because she's on social media and everyone looks prettier, or whatever problem she may express—what would you say to her?"

"You must raise your children with self-confidence and a strong sense of self so that they will be not swept away. Life is turbulent, and you must prepare your children for so many different sorts of things which can come their way. Open communication is so key. As I said a little while ago, be patient with your children, listen to them intently and really try to understand how they're feeling, even if it means asking them directly. Nip it in the butt, as they say."

"Bud, not butt."

"That's what I meant! I swear that's what I meant; it was a slip of the tongue."

"Elon Musk has a company called Neuralink. Eventually, they're going to implant chips into your head, and you will be able to just think about things to make them happen. How nervous does that make you?"

"I am always wondering about what is coming after I'm gone. I think that it's too crazy what is going to come. I think that humanity hopefully will not destroy itself. Although, I'm afraid it might. Hopefully technology brings more good than bad, and that we don't self-destruct! Robots are becoming more advanced; so is artificial intelligence. I don't really understand it, but the little I see, it's very scary."

"Geoffrey Hinton, the godfather of artificial intelligence, says he may have made a great mistake and resents it. Is it a little too late?"

"I'll be dead, so I'm safe," my mom joked. "It's like the atom bomb. You know Jews created the atom bomb."

"I wouldn't brag about that one, Mom," I warned her, half-joking.

"We'll keep that one between ourselves," she conceded. "But you can't stop progress in either a positive or negative way. Technology is here to stay, and it's only going to continue to evolve. And, unfortunately, human beings are crazy. I mean, look what's going on in Ukraine and the Mideast. They're killing each other with drones now."

"Does it make you sad to think that you won't be here to see the evolution of technology?"

"Definitely, very, very sad. Very sad that I will have to leave here soon. But mostly I'm sad that I won't be able to boss you and my grandchildren around anymore, that's the hardest part."

"What's that Steven Wright quote you just sent me? It's brilliant. You should put it into the book."

"First, you don't exist at all. Then you're born, and you live your whole life. Then you die. Then you go back to not existing again, forever. So, first you don't exist, then you exist. Then you don't exist. So, this whole thing is just an interruption from not existing" is what he joked.

"Is he Jewish? Can't be with the last name Wright, right?"

"Right about Wright," I answered even though I had no real idea. "Any final thoughts on technology?"

"It's very hard for me to have a final thought on anything, mainly because I like to keep talking. But it's especially hard when it comes to technology because we're still in its infancy. It's constantly evolving and constantly changing. But, then again, life itself is very much the same: always changing with the unexpected coming your way. So, my advice is stay prepared and evolve alongside the change."

Actual Voicemail from My Mom: May 14, 2022

Jo-el,

Your papa and mother are thinking of you and rooting for you.

May the force be with you.

But call us, and we'll be happy to talk to you.

Don't let anything get you down. It's not worth it. One day you'll be old and decrepit like your mama and papa.

[Click]

"DON'T CHOOSE A MISERABLE LIFE"

"**D**o you think I'll actually ever finish this book?" I asked my mother as we sat down to discuss something that's evaded me for close to fifty-four years: the power of positive thinking.

At this point I could see the proverbial light at the end of the tunnel, but I was perseverating about every possible circumstance that could keep me from typing that elusive last period. I could get a wicked case of writer's block, I could suffer an unexpected aneurysm (which would involve a whole lot more than just not finishing this masterpiece), or I could freeze from anxiety, simply unable to continue. In my mind, all these were viable possibilities for the seemingly insurmountable task of ever completing this opus.

"Do you think I'll ever finish this book?" I nagged at her.

"It must be exhausting to be so self-absorbed," my mom answered matter-of-factly, a response I've heard many times before. "I beg you to think about someone else. It must be so exhausting to only think about yourself all the time."

In fact, it is, because I'm perpetually exhausted. Each day feels like I'm slogging through waist-deep mud. It's nearly impossible for me to stay conscious between four and six each afternoon. Today was no different. My anxiety was gnawing at me again, and I needed some reassurance.

"Can you help calm me down? Say something soothing, please," I begged.

"I'm not a Klonopin, Joel."

"Anything comforting at all?"

"Yeah, don't choose a miserable life. Don't be an idiot. You're underground forever. I try to enjoy every minute of life."

"Why do I feel down and so stressed out?"

"Because you have the false thought that you have to be the prima donna of the world. I'm not into mood swings tonight, Joel."

My mom's headspace has always been an impenetrable steel trap. Mine is more like the hull of the *Titanic* after crashing into that now infamous iceberg. While my mom's mind is impervious to negativity, mine is constructed more like a sieve where untoward thoughts flow freely like lava from an active Kilauea volcano. We were mother and son, but how, I wondered, if our thought patterns were so incredibly different?

"Would you say that you're a positive person?" I asked, curious to see how she'd answer a question with such an obvious answer, while also wondering how long it would be before she'd sling her next insult at me.

"Many people live inside their head. But I don't like to do this, ever. I've always filled my head with knowledge. Even now, I hate to gaze at my navel and think about me. Even if I only have a spare ten minutes, I'm reading or googling something. I'm naturally curious and always want to know what's going on outside of me," she explained as she took aim at me. "You, on the other hand, love to run negative mental tapes through your mind."

"There's an entire cottage industry based on the power of positive thinking. Self-help gurus, authors, pastors, rabbis are all pushing it. Do you buy it?"

"Do you mean, can you train yourself to be a more positive person?"

"Forget training," I tell her impatiently. "Do you believe in the power of positive thinking?"

"One hundred percent I believe in it!"

"And would you say that you are a positive person?" I asked again.

"I consider myself a very positive person, but not by planning or by changing anything in my life. I think I was just born this way."

"People say, 'You survived the Holocaust. You must have a different makeup than the rest of us.' Do you have a different mental makeup?" I ask.

"Something interesting happened yesterday." My mom took her own detour. "I watched the show you did with Kay and Larry Woodcock whose grandson J. J. Vallow was murdered by his own mother, and Kay mentioned how she wasn't feeling emotions for a very long time after that."

"What's this have to do with my question?" It was a constant struggle to keep my mom focused on the subject at hand.

"I'm getting there. Not everything is a simple answer, Joel," she pushed back. "Kay Woodcock mentioned she now has a therapist she loves, and she's just beginning to feel sadness and pain and all the other emotions. But for a while she was cut off from herself."

I knew where my mom was going. She has always been able to, for better or worse, completely shut off her feelings and retreat into survival mode. I believe she learned this at four and a half when she went into hiding, while most other children that age are just beginning to learn to write.

"Emotionally, I think I have been cut off since childhood," my mom said, literally telling me exactly what I had just suspected. "I cut myself off from thinking or ruminating about anything negative. I just never allowed negativity to seep into my brain."

"Have you always disallowed negativity purely as a survival tactic? To get through hiding and to survive the untimely death of your son?"

"It probably started like that if I'm being honest," my mother admitted, "and then it also became part of how I deal with the world at large. This doesn't mean that I don't feel sadness or pain. But, if I had to guess, it's probably not to the same extent, or as acutely as some other people around me feel those same things."

"Are you a sociopath? Isn't that, by definition, sort of what a sociopath is?" I asked seriously, even though it was hard not to chuckle.

"I didn't say I don't feel guilt. I said I don't feel pain. I feel guilt, albeit to a much lower degree than you, for example. But I'm not a sociopath," my mom reiterated, as though she was insulted that I accused her of being labeled as such. "Every now and then I'll break a small rule like parking somewhere I shouldn't, but nothing bigger than that." She made it abundantly clear that she wasn't a sociopathic killer on the loose.

"I never said you were John Wayne Gacy or Jeffrey Dahmer," I added. "But you're definitely not as emotional as me."

"I'm guarded. Let's put it this way. I have protections up from childhood, and those became habit-forming over time."

"Do you think you're so guarded as a defense mechanism?"

"Yes. One hundred percent. It's self-protective and for self-preservation. It's because I am paranoid too. It's all very complex. My mother told me to be paranoid to protect myself from attacks. I love people, I really do. I consider myself an optimist, a people person. But I also don't trust people completely. It's all a complicated oxymoron to try to explain away."

"Do you trust me? One hundred percent?" I asked.

"No," my mom answered before I could even fully get the question out.

"Why not?" I laughed.

"I trust you ninety-nine percent. I think you are a little bit too self-absorbed for me. But I love you one hundred percent."

"Back to this notion of positivity," I rerouted us back on topic. "If someone asked you to describe your outlook on life, Mom, how would you answer?"

"Listen, now that I'm very close to death, and my life partner is on death's door, I am looking at it even a little differently than let's say a year ago when my husband was still functioning somewhat normally."

I could see her shifting into that protection mode right in front of my eyes. She was devastated by my father's current condition, but she would not let herself go there. Instead, she did what has helped her survive and flourish so long: she took a potentially negative thought and made it disappear.

"I look at this world as this tiny little ball. It's probably one of the smallest in the solar system. Okay, maybe not in the solar system, but certainly in the Milky Way."

What the hell is the difference between the solar system and the Milky Way? I wondered to myself, not wanting to interrupt her train of thought. If I verbalized this, she would've screamed at me to google it immediately. But I had a deadline looming.

Getting her thought across was more pressing than being perplexed about the topography of space.

"We're this nothing of a planet. It will eventually erupt like a volcano, or be hit by an asteroid; it's really a nothing of a place. And we're all here, as your father always would say 'for a blink of an eye.'"

I could tell she was fighting her emotions again. But she was pulling back on them like the reins on a horse.

"We can count back something like fifteen billion years. But I'm here for a blink of a time, a blink of an eye. And in this short time, I refuse to create drama. I will enjoy it as much as I can, even if it kills me. I just want to enjoy my visit here. And then, you know you are nowhere and nothing forever. My children might remember me for a few years and then they will eventually die too, and we will all be forgotten. I'm under no illusion."

Wow, I felt so much better. This is vintage "my mom." She always tells it like it is, no matter how harsh and real. It wasn't always so easy to deal with, and that's why sometimes I feel like I'm just surviving the survivor. But I couldn't imagine it or want it any other way. She continued.

"It's not cheerful, but it's reassuring, you know, that we should all just enjoy what is—whatever it is—that *is* happening to us, and you should enjoy every single day." She paused for a quick moment. "Did you get the article I sent?"

"What article?"

"You know, you're a real bitch. You never care to read what I send you. You send me stupid pictures of your dog Mabel Rose, but I send you something and you ignore it."

Some reading this may think it sounds harsh or funny, or both, but I don't even hear it. This is just our relationship, and it's not changing.

"I sent you an interesting article about this person who suggests that every day before you go to sleep, you should make an inventory of all the pleasant things that happened to you that day. It makes you have pleasant dreams."

"By the way, I had another dream last night that Bugs was cheating on me. I was late for my TV news live shot, and I needed help to google something, but my iPhone wasn't working. I couldn't get it to work. I looked for her everywhere to get help. And, when I finally found her, she was in bed fucking this other guy!"

"I really hope she cheats on you. You deserve it for all the stupid shit you put in your mind. You're visualizing it so much it will probably come to fruition, and I'll blame you, not her!" My mom took my wife's side. "Someone asked me why you call her Bugs. It's because of her big, beautiful eyes, right?"

"Yes, right," I answered dejectedly, wondering if she was out cheating on me while I was interviewing my mom. I snapped out of it and continued, albeit pissed off at my wife.

"There are all these snake oil salesmen selling positivity. You're a licensed therapist, so what are your thoughts on these people profiting from positivity?" I asked curiously.

"They are not snake oil salesmen. The self-help trend started in earnest around 1945, if I'm not mistaken, and it's been going strong ever since. Unless you're a Buddhist monk and were taught how to let everything flow like water and not let anything upset you, then you could probably benefit from these positivity peddlers."

"Why?"

"Because a big part of human existence is living with stress, agitation, and aggravation. If we're being honest, a lot of our lives are very difficult. I recently watched that documentary you recommended about chimpanzees on Netflix. They have it harder than we humans. They live in the rainforest of Uganda full of anxiety, worried about predators or being replaced by a bigger, stronger alpha male. They sit in the pouring rain, with thunder booming and lightning strikes, wondering if they're going to survive the night. They truly have difficult lives. I feel horribly for those chimpanzees. Don't make me watch that shit again. I told you I only want to be witness to happy things at my age."

Suddenly, I was the bad guy for suggesting to my mom that she watch a doc about chimps. It struck me in that moment that I became so good at working myself up from watching my mom do it so effortlessly.

"Okay, forget the chimps. Is there a simple path to happiness?"

"Well, there are many, many roads that lead to the same result. Religion works for some, the power of positive thinking works for others, but you need to find whatever works for you. I also believe some of it is genetic. I just saw Jane Fonda talk about her mother's suicide and that she too suffered from depression. It's why she became a fitness fanatic. It helped alleviate her depression and anxiety. I also think working out works wonders for people who struggle with their mental health."

"You have a pretty powerful mind. How do you think you developed it?"

"I don't have a powerful mind. You think I have a powerful mind. But whenever I come across a problem, I immediately think to myself how it can be resolved. It's a weird thing, but it's reflexive. I'm always looking for a solution."

"So, you do have a powerful mind?" I reiterated.

"Too many people, including you, play the role of victim." My mom saw an opening to make her point and rip me apart in the process. "Don't assume that you are a victim. I think you walk around during the day thinking you are a victim and at night you play the victim card too."

It was time to pivot slightly.

"I asked you about these people who push positivity. Let, let me just read a couple of quotes because I do my homework, and I come prepared."

"Don't always pat yourself on the back. You're writing this book and interviewing me for it, so you should come prepared!"

"Tony Robbins says, 'Identify your problems, but give your power and energy to solutions.' He also says, 'Your past does not equal your future,' and 'The path to success is to take massive, determined action,' and 'Live life fully while you're here. It's not knowing what to do; it's doing what you know,'" I read aloud and then asked, "Aren't these such obvious clichés?"

"They might be clichés. But they are very effective clichés. I'm very forward-looking. I really am very forward-looking. I'm not backward-looking. In fact, I oftentimes don't even remember things that happened in the past because I'm not focused on that. I'm focused on the future."

"This guy Tony Robbins, I don't even think he went to college, and he's impacted tens of millions of people. He's lucky because he's definitely getting a *New York Times* obituary. But do you consider him a snake oil salesman?" I asked again, hoping she'd say yes.

"No, I don't think he's a snake oil salesman at all. What the fuck does it matter that he went to or didn't go to college? He's smart and sells what he believes. And what does it matter that he's getting a *New York Times* obituary? He'll be dead and will never ever be able to read it. He'll be on this earth for a blink of an eye just like me and you."

I've always been obsessed with getting a *New York Times* obituary. After all, it's one of the true telltale signs you've made it in life. The only problem is you can never read it.

"Why do you think people need these kinds of trite sayings?"

"They are not trite. They are tested, trite, and true. You can think something will work out, and it'll work out. Or you can think something won't work out, and it definitely will not work out. It's like the story about the guy holding a bird, a little bird in his hand, you know?"

"No, I don't know!"

"The story is this guy is holding a tiny bird inside the, the palm…"

"The pedantic way you're telling me the story, it makes me want to crush the bird," I interrupted.

My comment was completely ignored. There wasn't even a scintilla of hesitation.

"The man asks his friend, 'What do you think? Will this bird live or die?' And the friend responds, 'How should I know? The bird is in your hands, and you determine its fate!'"

"I would've crushed it." I rushed to get it out. "What would you have done?"

"I one hundred percent would let the bird go. What did the bird ever do to me? But the point, schmuck, is you hold your own destiny, and in this case the bird's, in your own hand."

"Eckhart Tolle is another big name in the positivity racket. He says, 'To love is to recognize yourself in another,' and 'I have lived with several Zen masters, and all of them are cats.'"

"I know this might be controversial," my mom responded, "but I hate cats. I really don't trust them. And I have no idea what Zen masters and cats have to do with each other!"

I had no idea either. It went right over our collective heads.

"The famous Green Bay Packers football coach Vince Lombardi said, 'Confidence is contagious, but so is lack of confidence.' Do you agree?"

"Very smart," my mom conceded. "It's true because if you're a mother who has no confidence in how to raise her own children, you will raise children who don't have confidence either."

"Bruce Lee, the mixed martial artist and philosopher..."

My mom interrupted. "I know, I know Bruce Lee is the water guy."

While I remain a big sports fan, I really fell in love with martial arts beginning in my thirties. Don't get me wrong. I don't really do any, but I watch plenty. In fact, Dana White once invited me to try out as the UFC's second play-by-play guy. I had two weeks to prepare with legendary New York City sports anchor Bruce Beck, but it wasn't enough time. I've also met a lot of fighters, most of whom are smart and humble. There's something so raw about being able to be vulnerable enough to potentially get your ass kicked live on ESPN or pay-per-view. You'll never hear a fighter say, "I *think* I'm going to be champ one day." You *really* must believe in yourself because, as the great pugilist Nathan Diaz says, "It's either 'Kill or be killed!'"

"What's the Bruce Lee quote again?" my mom asked.

"He says, 'Be like water.' In other words, you need to adapt to whatever situation you find yourself in. But I have another of his quotes here. He says, 'Do not allow negative thoughts to enter your mind. For they are weeds that strangle confidence.'"

"Well, I love that. I love it," my mom responded. "The older I get the more I realize that there's no sense getting hung up on anything and especially not obsessing over it. You do have to be like water and adapt. I think negative thinking is also a habit."

"Expound, please. Again, this is a book, not an article for *Cosmo*."

"Do they still publish *Cosmo*? I used to love reading it when I'd get my hair done."

"How do you block out negativity?" I wanted to know if my mom had a secret.

"On my children's life," my mom invoked one of her favorite and most often used expressions to let the world know she was extra serious, "I'm telling you, and I'm not exaggerating, but since I can remember I knew we were all mortal and death was just a matter of time. We're all born with timers already ticking, so I made a conscious decision that I'm going to find a way to enjoy every day."

I had a rush of negativity and anxiety in that very moment. "Is anyone going to buy this book, let alone read it?"

"Let me tell you something. I warned you from the beginning that I'm a very average person and that nothing unusual would come from me." My mother seemingly took pride and, I daresay, enjoyment in exacerbating my concerns.

"I called you last night and I asked, 'Do you think this book will do well?' And you said, 'No, because I'm boring.' Meaning you!"

"Yes, I said that because I'm not interesting enough to have a book written about me. And I think it needs to have an angle. What do people get out of this book?"

"Hopefully life advice from *you*. But you say you haven't learned anything in life. That's what I'm trying to talk to you about right now!"

"What I learned in life is that everybody has to find their own way. The only thing I can do is tell you how I found my way, which I'm still trying to figure out at eighty-four."

"There's the old cliché: Do you see the glass half full or half empty?"

"Well, obviously I see it half full," my mom answered without a second thought, adding, "Even though I know it's half empty, I still choose to see it half full."

"Why?"

"Because going through life with a half-empty glass would be a very disappointing way to live."

"Well, I just read a quote about how confidence is contagious. I tend to see things a bit half empty," I told my mom, surprising no one. "I worry that this book's not going to be too good."

"You're always busy covering all your bases. If you think it's half empty, it's true, it's half empty. But what good does it do for you?" my mom said, never tiring of teaching.

A while back, my mom told me to read another article about stress being addictive. I just made the mistake of admitting I'd only read the headline.

"You're a hollow head idiot. Why do I bother sending you anything? Yes, I don't believe it. I know it to be true. You're a perfect example because *you* can't live without a modicum of stress in your own life."

"Why am I a stress addict?"

"It's like adrenaline in a certain way. It's familiar. You've relied on it your entire life. It's a dopamine hit for you, and you don't get it, you crave it. Why? Bottom line is it's because you're dumb. You're just not *that* smart, I'm sorry to say," my mom answered despite not being sorry at all. She has always loved to rip me apart to underscore the importance of her points.

"So, what would you say to someone who wants to know the best way to live their life?"

"Well, I wouldn't say anything definitive. I'd speak to them and try to find out more about them and their situation. There's no 'one size fits all' solution, and I'm not even sure there's a solution at all to anything in this crazy world of ours."

"Mom, you just told me about a self-made billionaire who still says that he's anxious and worries. What would do you say to him?"

"Well, he didn't seem to be consumed by it. He seemed to be doing quite well and acting proactively. I think anxiety is part of everybody's life to a degree. But it's the level of anxiety one experiences. Both you and your father have been paralyzed by anxiety at times. This billionaire worries too. Money never brings happiness. It can just make some things, like paying the bills, easier. It probably adds more problems than it eliminates."

"Let's talk about someone that's very important to you: me," I told my mom as she rolled her eyes at me and pretended to vomit. "Why *do* you think that I have such high anxiety? Why do I wake up worried every day? I mean, I was given a lot of love and support from you and Dad."

"You know what Roy, your father, would say, if he could speak right now?"

"What?"

"He'd say it's because you're stupid. No other reason than that you're stupid."

"Okay, well he can't speak right now. So what do you say? Why am I so anxious? Why am I worried about money? Why am I worried about my book? Why am I worried about my podcast's success?"

"I think it's your enormous ego. You think that you are so unbelievably phenomenal that your first book will be a bestseller, that you should be making the most money, and you know whose fault it is? It's mine for spoiling you rotten. I gave you the impression that you're better than you are. Here's another saying you should learn, fast: 'Happy is the man who is happy with his own lot.'"

I'd hit a nerve with my mom. She really felt responsible for my anxiety, faulting herself for propping me up too much in life.

"It's my fault that you think you're hot shit." She continued, "Everybody carries their own burden in life. But, unlike the advice your father gave you to mind your own business, you never do! You are constantly looking over your shoulder to see what others are doing. You're metaphorically constantly comparing penis size. Just mind your fucking business and write this book and don't worry if anyone will ever read it. That's not your problem."

"To me, one of the true signs of success—" I began to explain before being cut off.

"Success? Success?" my mother repeated incredulously. "Even the word 'success' is such a sick term. You know why? What is success? Define success…"

"Um, achieving what you want to achieve," I answered as we swerved off the topic of positivity into what we do best: arguing.

"Success isn't ideal if your intention is to murder somebody," my mom snapped at me.

"Well, you were telling me about this anxious billionaire, obviously impressed by his money," I battled back.

"Successful? On what level? How?" she barked!

"He made billions!"

"Does he have inner peace?"

"I have no fucking idea!"

"Inner peace I'll concede is a form of success. I'll give you that, dummy," my mom said.

Dummy isn't a word she used often, if ever. So, admittedly, that took me by surprise.

"So how do you acquire inner peace since you're bringing it up?" I said as I looked for another simple answer to an incredibly complex question.

"Google it. You're on your damn phone so much it must have all the answers," she answered angrily.

"Instead of putting me down, I'm asking you. How does one achieve inner peace?"

"I'm not putting you down. I don't have your ego. I do not expect this book to be a bestseller. I'd be happy if five people read it. You want five hundred million people to read it."

"In fairness to me, I said one million."

"We have different levels of expectations. You call me 'Mediocrates.' I'd rather be happy and mediocre than exceptional and unhappy. So, you choose how you want to live your life!"

"I'll ask again: What *is* inner peace, and how do you get it?"

"I told you. It's being happy with your lot and not expecting more or desiring more than you deserve."

"I don't love that answer."

"Your father is so sick. Should I dwell on that? No, I shouldn't. Instead, I'm grateful we had sixty-four beautiful years together. That's success. That's inner peace. There's your answer. Stay married to your wife for sixty-four years."

"I'd be a hundred and six. I got married too late. It's not fair!" I screamed into a vacuous hole.

"By the way," my mom offered, "I find billionaires very sad."

"Why?"

"In life, there are two real tragedies: getting what you want and not getting what you want."

"So, what's the happy medium?"

"I have no idea."

We had taken ourselves far off the path of positivity.

"Let me circle back here. Forget the rest, for now. How do you stay so positive?" I asked my mom as we both worked to calm ourselves down. Her answer illustrated that she was still agitated and annoyed by me.

"I think you are in such an unhappy direction because you're constantly looking over your shoulder at others. I'm saying this to you without any anger or any resentment." This meant she, in fact, was filled to the brim with anger and resentment, as she continued, "I'm disappointed with you because you do not come from a family like this. You are constantly monitoring what other people have, and you are constantly jealous and green with envy."

"I'm trying to get us back to the subject of positivity!"

"And I'm answering you, asshole! But you refuse to listen. If you want to be positive, then stop looking at what others are doing and focus on what *you* are doing, moron!"

I was again unfazed by her rising temper, anger, and disappointment. I just wanted to know how to get there. "How do I do it?"

"Inch by inch." She repeated, "Inch by inch."

"Fine," I settled for her answer. "If you're a negative person, can you become a positive person? Do I have hope?"

"Of course, you can!"

"How?"

"Just give up your negativity. Have the strength to let go of the negative. Don't be a pussy," she added for shock value, despite all the potential for shock being drained out of me years ago.

"But how can I really change into a positive person?"

"It's like righting a ship. It takes a while. You need to be steady and get yourself a good therapist!"

"I can't afford a therapist," I mumbled helplessly.

"Then stay miserable for the rest of your life."

Actual Voicemail from My Mom: *January 3, 2022*

I'm at the dentist with Roy, and I wanted to talk to you about, about practical stuff.

So, I can be reached, and I want to hear from you.

I love you. Have a good evening, I mean, good morning.

And remember, your mama and papa love you most in the world.

"SIRI, WHAT IS LOVE?"

L
ike so many other days, I'd wrap up the podcast and race over to Miami Jewish to visit my dad. This book is mainly about how my mother's crushingly honest life advice helped shape me. But the other half of that parental equation, of course, is my father. He was always the yin to my mom's yang. She's excitable, to say the least, with a tongue like a lizard always lashing out at you. My dad, on the other hand, has always been a calming, soothing voice of reason. When I was anxious, which was every day, he'd always say something to help alleviate my stress. Whenever I'd get ready to take an exam in high school or college, he'd tell me something very counterintuitive: enjoy it. When it came to finances, my dad would remind me "it's only money." Now he was lying on an air mattress, to help prevent bed sores, in a place where all the residents are teetering between this world and whatever comes next.

"How are you, Dad?" I asked, pulling up a chair beside him, as Jewish Broadcasting Service blared on the television. JBS is a public access cable channel based in New York City and universally loved by Jews primarily over the age of eighty-five, at least by my calculations. My dad just stared into space, no longer even acknowledging my presence. JBS aired old interviews with even older Jews like Jackie Mason, who happens to be so old now that he's no longer even alive.

My mom got furious at me the other day when I told her she looked a bit like Jackie Mason after her hairdresser went a little too heavy on the red dye. I preferred my mom blonde.

"He smiled today," one of the nurse's assistants told me as she came in to check my dad's feeding tube, looking for something, anything, to console me.

My mom walked in a few minutes after me.

"How is he?" she asked.

Her red hair was still jolting.

"I can't beat him in a staring contest anymore," I answered sarcastically, as we both watched him staring, expressionless, at absolutely nothing.

I began to tear up.

"Did you corner the market on misery?" my mom asked.

"No, I cornered the market on having a father for fifty-three years who can no longer speak and will never be able to give me advice again," I snapped back.

"He can hear you," my mom cautioned. "Remember you're the first one ever to lose a father," she added bitingly, underscoring the harshness of reality.

How the hell did she know he could still hear? There's an old joke: What's the difference between God and doctors? God doesn't know everything. My mom was just like a doctor thinking she knows everything. Could he still really hear everything?

My dad's room was sparse with just an old wooden dresser drawer on which a small flat-screen TV sat, which looked more like an early model computer monitor than a television. My children's get-well card hung on the barren white wall next to the pale pink sliding curtain used to divide the room from his much younger neighbor who was also drooling—except his oral secretions were from early onset Alzheimer's.

My dad, who had always been thin, was now "Auschwitz survivor" frail. His once handsome face was now sunken in with his cheekbones protruding. You could see the outline of his femur bone beneath his paper-thin skin. I could connect the tip of my thumb and middle finger around his ankle with an inch to spare. His face was blank, all his expression gone, with a bit of spittle on each corner of his mouth. The din of discordant sounds of hospital equipment played like Muzak in the background.

"I love you, Dad," I uttered before tears began flooding from my eyes. I was overtired, emotional, and terrified at the thought of losing the most important man in my life, and how it would invariably affect the most important woman in my life, the one now trying to pick a fight with me because I was being too emotional about my dad's final days on planet earth.

John F. Kennedy Jr. once said you don't really become an adult until your parents pass away. I never want to become an adult. I'm fine in my current arrested state of development at fifty-three.

I looked over at my mom, who was now also quietly crying.

"Let's go for a walk," I suggested. She agreed.

Outside his wing of Miami Jewish, which is a sprawling campus, is one of the biggest trees I've ever seen. We were told by some nurses' aides it was 350 years old. We nicknamed it "the Elephant" because its roots resembled the beautiful animal's trunk. Its branches and leaves were so enormous that they became a playground for the local squirrels and feral cats, and a stage for the birds to dance upon. My mom loves elephants and was equally passionate about this tree, which was the only uplifting resident of Miami Jewish.

It was the perfect time to ask my mom about the universally most important topic: love.

"How do you define love?" Both of our sets of eyes were still red and watery from seeing my dad's withering condition. I wish he was still strong like the elephant tree.

"You just asked the most impossible question," my mom remarked. "How do I define love?"

"Yes, that was the question."

"You know people do not get any smarter with age, I've told you," my mom reiterated. "I still don't really, really, really know what love is. But the strange thing is I think your four-year-old son, Judah, knows exactly what love is. It's a fleeting emotion. I'm not sure how fleeting exactly, but we all experience it at some point, even our dogs do."

"Why do you think Judah understands love, but you're not convinced that you do, despite so much more life experience?"

"Because when he marches off to school he always says, 'I love you.' And he knows what he's feeling at that moment. He feels primal emotion, which you can't see, smell, or feel. It's just something that binds us all. I don't know if it's instinctual, imprinted from birth, or what. The definition of love has also changed throughout human history. During the time of the troubadours, for example, they would write long sonnets, but the sexual part would not be included in the love. It was only the emotion. Love is also a very multifaceted word. In different cultures there are sometimes seven or eight different words for love. You love your dog, you love your wife, you love your children, you love your parents, you love your friends. But these are all different, varying emotions."

"You love chocolate," I said to my mom, who was nervously nibbling on a piece of Swiss chocolate.

"I hate when I bite into it, and there's raspberry. It's like my whole experience is ruined," she added in an annoyed, dejected tone. "I think the word 'love' is as abused as it comes, yet it's as beautiful an emotion as there is."

"You still haven't defined what love *is*," I reminded my mom.

"If I would take a bullet for you is how I define it. Nothing more, nothing less."

"Would you take one for me?" I asked pointedly.

"If there's someone who loves you more than I love you, I don't know who it is," my mom said with another tear rolling down her cheek. "I've reached the peaks of the peaks. Americans like to say I'd stand in front of a bullet for you. And like I just mentioned, I'd do that for you without thinking. I hate to use these crass analogies. But it's the truth, and it's what I would do for you."

I felt just a little bit safer in this unpredictable world that my father was very predictably going to leave too soon.

"Do you remember the first time you loved someone or something?" I asked.

"Yes, I remember consciously loving my Grandmother Najyi. I loved everything about her. She was fat and soft and smelled nice and would do absolutely anything for me. She would've taken a bullet for me."

That same pesky teardrop began to form in my mom's eye as she thought more about her Grandma Najyi.

"She was the most loving grandmother to me. She would have done anything for me, and I would have done anything for her. We lived together when I was very young, and we had a common enemy: my mother." My mom laughed. "We were just very close, very tight. She was bright. She was one of those people who could multiply multi-digit numbers in her head. She was so smart and read a lot too. But she had a poor self-image because she was homely looking and often neglected by her husband."

"Would you say that you love elephants? And, if so, how does that love differ than your love for Grandma Najyi?"

"Well, for me, love includes a certain element of protection. There's a certain vulnerability related to love whereby you want to watch over whoever it is whom you love. When it comes to elephants, I absolutely do love them, and they seem to love each other. I saw a documentary recently where a herd of elephants were walking and, suddenly, a baby fell into a ravine. The mother raced over and pulled her baby out with her trunk. If that's not love, then I don't what is. They're also known for their memories. When your father and I visited Thailand, it was amazing to watch the elephants with their little twelve-year-old human handlers. They were like brothers, like family, despite being two completely different species. It was so beautiful."

"Do you love this tree?" We both looked up at the giant tree, Miami Jewish's most beloved resident.

"This tree must be three hundred and fifty years old, like they say, because it's so huge and majestic. Think of all the history she's seen." My mom would always assign a female gender to inanimate objects she anthropomorphized. "It's a very touching tree. I could cry looking at this tree, so I do love it. I'd give it a hug, but then I'd be a tree hugger."

"Now, onto the real love of your life: me." I chuckled. "No, I mean your husband. Did you fall in love with him right away? Do you believe in love at first sight?" I wanted to know her thoughts on the age-old cliché.

"I was attracted to him at first sight. He was tall, dark, and handsome. But I'm not sure I'd describe that as falling in love.

Plus, love is not just about sleeping with someone, although your father and I loved to do it a lot..."

"All right, spare me the details, and stick to the subject," I urged her.

"The truth is I have no idea what love at first sight even means. It's something you see more in the movies than in real life. It's not enough to just be physically attracted. You must also understand each other in other, more complex ways. Intelligence, for example, doesn't need to be equal, but you both need to match each other intellectually to a degree. And Roy, your father..."

"I know Roy is my father. Why do you always qualify it for me?"

"Just in case you forget. And you're usually not listening to me anyway, so I want to make sure I'm being clear," she sniped. "Your father would always say your neuroses need to match too. They shouldn't be the same, but the neurotic tendencies should complement each other. Imagine two of you?"

"I'd be more concerned about two of you," I responded. "If I had two parents relentlessly screaming at me, it would be bordering on child abuse!"

"What, Joel?" my mom screamed for dramatic effect, instantly raising my blood pressure and heart rate, despite her poor attempt at humor.

"Would you describe Roy as the love of your life?"

"Well, it would be very hard to describe him as anything less since I spent about sixty-three years with him."

"You could've both just been bored, filling some time," I joked. "What do you love about each other? More importantly, what do you love so much about him?"

"Everything. But, at the same time, it's important to point out that nobody's perfect."

"Except for me."

My mom ignored me.

"Roy has his craziness, but I love him in spite of it or because of it; I'm still not even sure. My love for him, like you and your sister, is unconditional. Even now, that he's having accidents and will occasionally make in his diaper, and it stinks like shit, literally, I want to help him; I want to take care of him."

"So, is cleaning shit from a diaper true love? Because, if so, I'm madly in love with all three of my children," I pointed out.

"No, but that is extreme proof to me because when I think about it, I realize there is nothing that can stop me from loving him. If he has an accident, I clean it up, I clean myself up, and then I get right back into bed next to him."

"Earlier, you defined love as being willing to take a bullet for someone. Would you take a bullet for Dad?"

"No, probably not," she responded so deadpan I'm not sure if she meant it.

"So, you didn't love him *that* much?"

"I loved him up to the point of taking a bullet for him. Maybe it's because I've never had to take a bullet for him. I am being very honest with you. I think I would only take a bullet for you or your sister, Arden."

"What about Grandma Najyi?"

"No."

"Would you take the bullet for me before you took it for Arden?" I loved to challenge her.

"No!"

"So, what is love?" I dug deeper.

"This is probably the most difficult topic for me. It's the most incomprehensible for my limited brain capacity because I simply cannot absorb it. The entire world turns on love, but so few people really know what it is, if any."

"How so?"

"I don't understand life. That's what it comes down to. I don't understand life because I don't understand the most base concept: love. Movies are made about love, and books are written about it. Love was an integral part of Greek tragedies, and the Torah discusses love in-depth. But what is it, exactly? Maybe google it."

"What?"

"Ask Sari!" my mom nudged me, looking for the answer.

"It's Siri."

"Whatever the fuck her name is. Ask her!"

I obliged her. She is my mother, after all.

"Siri, what is love?" I asked my iPhone 15.

"As I understand it, love refers to a deep, tender, ineffable feeling of affection and solicitude," Siri answered immediately, seemingly very confident in her answer.

"What is solicitude?" my mom wanted to know. "Ask Sari!"

"Siri, not Sari. This book is your take on life, not Siri's."

"Well, ask her about love again. I didn't catch it entirely."

"As I understand it," Siri repeated, with a hint of aggravation in her voice, having just been asked the same question, "love refers to a deep, tender, ineffable feeling of affection and solicitude."

"Okay, so now ask her what the definition of Jewish love is?"

"I can answer that. It's worrying together 'til death do us part. Do you worry about Dad?"

"Yes, I've always worried about your father. I feel sorry for him too."

"Why?"

"Because he gets anxious for no good reason. The sad irony is now I don't think he's anxious because he's too sick to worry. I just wish he realized this was a wasted emotion while he was still healthy."

"It's a good thing I never get anxious," I added sarcastically. "What about your love for your children, your daughter and your son? How is this love different than the love for your husband or for an elephant?"

"Well, I wouldn't sleep with an elephant, unlike your father."

"Would you breastfeed an elephant?" We were both a little loopy by now.

My mom let out an audible laugh. It was rare for either of us to truly catch the other off guard.

"I think my love for Roy was all-encompassing. We did everything for each other without giving up our individual selves. However, I know you won't believe this, but I was never one hundred and ten percent trusting of him. After fifty years, I began to feel a little bit safer and less vulnerable."

"Why were you distrusting of his trust?"

"I have no real idea. He's always been faithful, as far as I know, and very, very loving. I may need to extend the window of time. Maybe fifty years isn't long enough," she pondered out loud. "I loved him as a lover and as a friend, and as a very decent human being. Can you tell me a single person he ever had a fight with during his life, ever?" she asked rhetorically.

"Enough of Dad. It's time to get back to me. How is your love for your children different than your love for your husband?"

"It's like the documentary you begged me to watch on those chimps. My love for my children is pure animal instinct. I'm protective over both of you. I don't like anyone to fuck with my children. That's where it crosses the line."

"What wouldn't you do for your children?" I hoped the answer was nothing.

"Well, I put up with a lot of your crap. Yours more than Arden's. But, in fairness, I annoy you two a lot also. I give you suggestions about what to do about different things. But I do it out of anxiety to try to protect you. Some of what I do is for my own ego. I think it's all very, very complex. There are so many elements to a mother's love for her children. It's like a cake that you have to add a lot of different ingredients to give it the perfect taste. I'm a horrible baker, by the way. But it's so complicated in my own mind, in my own brain, what love is. I actually like Siri's definition. It makes perfect sense, even though I'm still not exactly sure what solicitude is. Ask her what love is one more time, for me."

"Jesus Christ. Siri, what is love?"

"As I understand it, love refers to a deep, tender, ineffable feeling of affection and solicitude."

"Okay, ask her the definition of affection. I'm curious what she says." My mom really wanted to know.

"I'm changing the title of the book to *Surviving Siri*. What is the definition of affection?" I complied with my mom's request.

"Affection is a gentle feeling of fondness or liking," she answered as though she was getting increasingly annoyed.

"Some people might say you don't love your kids because you scream at them a lot. What would you say to that?"

"Boy, they don't get it. It's the exact opposite."

"When I reprimand you on our podcast, people think I am a terrible son."

"Not everyone gets everyone else. I think we have a stronger love for each other than most. But sometimes it's misinterpreted because we both have the tendency to get too excited."

"Do you think you would really take a bullet for me or Arden?"

"Yes!"

"Would you still take one?"

"I'm getting a little too old for that now. The situation would have to play out for me to see how I would react. Plus, my reflexes are very slow now."

We laughed.

"Would you still stroll me in a stroller? My legs are sore from the gym."

"You're sick. It's not even funny, Joel."

"Youth is really wasted on the young. Judah Mac doesn't know how good he has it with me carting his ass around."

"One of my biggest mistakes, which I regret greatly, is spoiling you the way I did. I indulged you so much."

"Do you really love chocolate?" Both my mom and I have an unhealthy addiction to sweets, particularly chocolate.

"It's a reward system. And it's also a mild tranquilizer for me."

"Have you always felt loved?"

"Yes, I always felt loved, especially you and your sister's love and, of course, Roy's love. But now I'm really missing his because he can no longer communicate it."

"And does the absence magnify what it once was?"

"More than you know."

"Does STS Nation give you any solace? We've built up a really warm, caring community around our podcast, which is over one hundred thousand people strong. Do they help lift you up?"

"I have a confession," my mom openly admitted. "I love the attention. And the podcast gives me a lot of attention. The community is truly amazing. They write to us and tell us how much they appreciate our work..."

"My work is greater than yours, of course..."

"That goes without saying, but their love for me might be a little bit greater." My mom smirked.

"What do you love about the attention?"

"I love that they care about me. And I think they truly do care." My mom stared at my face.

"What do you have on the side of your mouth there?" she asked.

"I have no idea."

"You have some food stuck on your beard. And your beard looks like shit because it makes you look at least ten years older. Shave it! How many times do I need to beg you to shave it?"

"Wow, you really do love me!"

"Do you know what your wife's definition of love is?"

"What?"

"I'm asking!" I was sure my mom had the answer to that question.

"No, I have no idea. But it seems to be working out so far."

One thing my mom has always loved are curveball questions.

"So how do you sum up love?" I asked, hoping to find some closure to such a mysterious human emotion.

"It's one of the great mysteries of the universe. It's so hard to define. And everybody experiences it differently, I think. And when one is deprived of love, it's even clearer what love is because it's easier to define the lack of it than love itself."

Actual Voicemail from My Mom: March 7, 2022

I wanted to talk to you. Your father is not doing so well. He's not dying, but it's not great right now.

I started to go to the, the Miami Jewish, uh, to see Roy.

And there was such a wind, I couldn't open the door to the garage, and it was like the palm trees were bending.

And I came back up. And now I feel very bad for Roy.

It's your mother, by the way.

"MY HUSBAND IS MY LIFE"

THE NIGHT BEFORE...

"I think you're going to see a fight over the narrative," one of our #BestGuests warned #STSNation, our true crime community, during the lead-up to Lori Vallow Daybell's trial.

She's the demented so-called "Doomsday" mom from Arizona who was ultimately convicted in a Boise, Idaho courtroom of savagely murdering her two beautiful young children and her husband's ex-wife, leaving a pile of bodies in her wake.

She said she believed zombies had overtaken her children, and so they needed to be eliminated.

"The defense will make it as black and white as they can. Lori's going to try to beguile the jury, just like she had done with her followers," one of our #BestGuests continued.

My mom was co-hosting that night, as she does every Sunday evening, and when asked about her final thoughts, my mom simply said, "I love #STSNation!"

My mom has always known how to play to a crowd. Maybe she should've been president. #STSNation flooded the chat with their usual adoration for the matriarch of our true crime program, which was now consistently getting well over one million eyeballs per month on YouTube alone.

"Great show! Karm, you're wonderful," read one message. Another just wrote "Karm" with a row of heart emojis following it. A viewer from Tasmania, of all places, typed, "Love you Karm!"

Again, my mom, who has become this cult of personality, responded back, "We are all love, no hate!"

The chat room blew up. It was our version of Bruce coming out for an encore.

Then there was a final question from #STSNation: "How's your husband, Karm?" We were a tight-knit group, and our community knew my father was not in great shape now, just existing in Miami Jewish, but not really living anymore.

My mother's response was both simple and powerful: "My husband is my life."

None of us knew it then, but the very next morning, less than twelve hours later, my father's life ended, and my mother's life was inexorably changed.

THE MOST DIFFICULT CONVERSATION...

My mom and I sat down to discuss the most difficult chapter in this book: death.

I had been pestering her for weeks to make time to discuss my dad's passing. I knew this was harder for her than losing her father to the Auschwitz gas chamber, or her stepfather to Parkinson's, or her son to a genetic disease.

My father was truly my mom's life. Over sixty-three years they grew into one, and now she was suddenly ripped in two.

Even in all her obvious pain, she squeezed out some humor. "I'm dying to discuss death."

"It's been a few weeks since Dad passed. Why are you 'dying' to discuss death tonight?"

"Because you have OCD and won't leave me alone. So, let's get it over with," she admitted.

My mom and I were in Israel for my niece's (her granddaughter Hana's) wedding. I knew this was the place for a discussion about death because my mom's emotions were so raw in Israel.

We had just returned from a brand-new Tel Aviv museum called ANU, which means "us" in Hebrew, and it really impacted my mom.

"Why did you begin to cry at the museum?"

"I had an epiphany," she said, her eyes welling up with tears despite her attempt at showing unflappable strength. "Your father died, and I'll die soon. So many others have already died—all those brilliant minds we saw at the museum today who helped build Israel with their ingenuity. So many of them are dead too. But I realized today, for the first time, that Israel will never die. We come and go, but the state is here to stay if people still walk this earth. We are such a smart, strong, resilient people. For more than five thousand years, the world has tried to eliminate us, and they have always failed and will continue to do so. We are here to stay."

Neither of us had any idea a war would break out just a few months later illustrating life's unrelenting unpredictability.

There was nothing more important to her than Israel, except maybe my father. After what she experienced during World War Two, it was only Israel that could pacify my mom and give her some sense of security in a very insecure world. My father gave her that too.

"You were exposed to death at an unfortunately young age. I, on the other hand, never really experienced a death close to me until Dad."

"Your dog Mabel died," my mom said matter-of-factly, but she meant it sincerely.

I had Mabel Rose before I met my wife or had any of my three children. She died a few weeks shy of seventeen, just a few months before my father. It still gutted me. The hardest part was that she passed overnight at the emergency veterinarian clinic during the few hours I had left her side to get some sleep. I was incredulous the next morning when the doctor called to tell me she was gone. How could I not have been there in her biggest time of need? Early the next morning, sobbing uncontrollably, I lay beside her stiff, cold body. How could I ever forgive myself? I began to tear up too.

"Losing a dog, especially Mabel, is hard. I know how much you loved that dog," my mom comforted me as I felt even more guilt discussing the death of my beloved Mabel Rose instead of my father. I didn't want my mom accusing me of making our death conversation about me, which I knew I was teetering dangerously close to doing, so I reeled the conversation back into my father. My mom was staring out into space.

"You look almost dead right now," I said nonchalantly, trying to break up the intensity of the conversation we were now in the middle of.

"That's because I'm talking about death," my mom responded with her distant gaze uninterrupted.

THE WORST DAY OF OUR LIVES...

"So, what was it like for you when we were summoned to Miami Jewish the morning Dad passed? They called to say he wasn't doing well. What do you remember about that morning?" I asked in rapid-fire succession.

"Well, as you know, they called, and it was about seven a.m. I knew the end was coming because he was throwing blood clots in his legs, which at any time could have traveled up to his lungs, where they would block his arteries and kill him. So, they had to give him blood thinners, which was also a losing proposition because I knew that he could bleed out from the blood thinners. I knew that this was the endgame. He had lost a lot of weight. I don't think he was in pain, but he was no longer living. He was just wasting away in his bed."

We were both tearing up. This was already an emotional mess of a conversation. Part of me wondered if I should be pushing my mom right now. I told myself this was important for both of us to discuss.

"Were you ready?"

"No one's ever ready. And even though he was going to turn ninety, you're never old enough to die. Never old enough. It's never ever enough time. With that said, I had a lot of time to prepare mentally. The only thing I couldn't prepare myself for is Roy grasping for breath."

"It's gasping, not grasping."

"Oh, fuck off, Joel."

I knew that would lighten the mood a touch.

"I just didn't want to watch him gasping for air for a long time. When they called me, they said he was kind of gasping for air. That part I knew I couldn't handle."

"When you get to Miami Jewish that morning, what did you see?"

"Well, it was in that little hospital, I think it's called Douglas Gardens, which is attached to Miami Jewish, which was recently renovated, and I see the nurse Eddie," my mom continued.

Eddie is one of those guys that make you wonder about yourself. He's not into money or celebrity; that gene doesn't exist in Eddie the nurse. He works in one of the most depressing places you can imagine with only one concern: how to help people in their last years, days, and, as we found out, even in their final minutes and seconds. If our society was more focused on lifting up people like Eddie the nurse, we'd be a much better place.

"Eddie the nurse was amazing," I emphatically told my mom. "He had hope until the very end. He wouldn't stop working on Dad."

I was already at Miami Jewish when my mom arrived. My father was really struggling, and Eddie's singular focus was how to help alleviate any possible suffering, while hoping he could restabilize my dad.

"Wasn't it amazing Eddie the nurse still seemed to have hope?" I asked Mom.

"He didn't hope. He worked," my mom corrected me. If you haven't figured it out by now, my mom is blunt. And this situation was no different. She didn't want me to conflate hope with a superhero nurse's efforts in the waning moments of my dad's life. I tried to push back.

"Hold on a second," I said. "Miami is filled with flamboyant Ferrari-driving, Prada-shoe-wearing, money-fueled egos, but this guy was a saint. He was doing everything he could to help Dad, including wiping the spittle from the corners of his mouth. What do you think of that kind of person in those moments? Where do you place a guy like Eddie in the human hierarchy?"

"He has a terrific sense of humor, very funny, despite the morbid nature of his work. During the eight months your dad was at Miami Jewish, I always joked with Eddie, and he got a little annoyed that I would never let him move Roy to hospice. I think he thought we were hopelessly hopeful."

"He should be making a hundred and twenty-five million dollars over five years, not some guy that can hit a baseball, which is just a bunch of rubber bands bundled together in a leather casing, with a wooden bat," I argued.

"I agree, but that's not reality because morons like you watch baseball," she laughed. "I thought he was a very caring, smart, experienced nurse who excelled at being able to compartmentalize difficult moments. When I was a social worker, for example, if someone threatened suicide, I would block it from my mind after our session. Self-preservation sometimes requires this."

That fateful day, March 27, 2023, my dad weighed half of what he once did at around eighty-five pounds. He was flat on his back, with his eyes and cheeks sunken so deep into his face that he was barely recognizable. One of the sweetest men I ever knew was just moments from never being able to express that sweetness again.

"Lisandra, your dad's caretaker, was also there," my mom reminded me. "His breathing was so labored. He was having terrible difficulty just trying to get oxygen into his lungs."

"What was it like for you to see the man you've been with for all those years in that most deteriorated state?"

"He was in various states of that deterioration for the last eight months," my mom answered matter-of-factly. "The day they brought him into the emergency room, he had to be intubated. Doctors told us then that he might not make it through the night, remember?"

The night my father was initially admitted to the hospital, I rode with him in the ambulance as famed Collins Avenue in

Miami Beach parted like the Red Sea for the first responders to get through. I thought for a moment that I could've used lights and a siren for all those years I battled New York City traffic. Just a day or so later, my mom, so flustered by the newness of his rapidly declining health, ran toward him falling and dislocating her own shoulder in the process. It was a sad mess.

"It was a terrible experience," my mom said. "The hospital was always cold with those fluorescent lights, and it was just a very unpleasant place. But I had this compulsion. I told myself I would never, never ever miss a day visiting him. You guys had to drive me at first because my shoulder was in such bad shape. I was in a sling for weeks."

My mom kept that obsessive promise. I can't recall a single day where she didn't visit the man who was, quite literally, her other half, devastated but not broken by the sadness of the situation.

"He deteriorated progressively. Cognitively he had already begun to slide downhill, as he was having trouble remembering his own grandchildren's names and where they lived. My mother's death was so easy compared to this. I'm very good at avoiding horrible feelings," my mom admitted, "but this was *really* horrible."

"Losing your mom was really easier than losing your husband?" I reiterated the point my mom had just made to make sure I heard her correctly.

"I saw my mother a few hours after she died, and it was not so terrible. She was ninety-eight and a half. I was living on a different continent. I loved her a lot, but, if I'm being honest, she didn't leave a big hole in my life. That's because at that point she wasn't filling a major role in my life. We lived across the ocean from each other, and even though we spoke often, I no longer depended on her."

In that moment, I had a flood of thoughts wondering how I'd ever be able to survive the survivor sitting before me. She was such a powerful, overwhelming force who guided me through every twist and turn life delivered. How could I lose this person and still navigate this harsh, scary world without her?

"Roy was my rock," my mom continued, snapping me out of my own self-absorbed fear. "Imagine you are anchored and suddenly the anchor disappears, and you are free-floating in the universe emotionally and every other way imaginable."

"You just stole that line from me!" I snapped at my mom.

Whenever I'd think of her demise, it would make me feel like I was spinning backward through space without gravity to hold me down. I had expressed this sentiment to my mom a lot in the past, which was always met with disgust and disappointment that I could be so weak. I also told her the thought of losing her would feel like climbing up the side of a gravel mountain with nothing to grab onto and nowhere to gain my footing.

"I thought I stole that line from someone," she confessed. "I just didn't remember that it was from you. It sounds better coming from me anyway."

"How does losing Dad compare to your father being gassed in Auschwitz? I know you said Dad's loss was harder, but how was it different?"

"I lost my father when I was five years old, and I'm still furious about it. You have no idea how furious I *really* am about it," she said as her voice filled with anger.

Like so many times before, my mom would stare out into the distance when speaking about her father, like she was trying to reel in memories that had drifted so far afield.

"When I was five years old, I had dreams of burning houses down and real frightening nightmares," my mom shared.

I had never ever heard about this before. I thought my mom was incapable of still shocking me.

"What do you mean burning houses down?"

"What do you mean, what do I mean? It's what I just said! I had frequent dreams that I was burning homes down in our neighborhood."

I understood my mother was angry to her core about losing her father in the animalistic way she did. But how did arson become part of all this death and darkness?

"They burned my father. Those fucking piece of shit Nazis incinerated the man I loved more than anyone in the world, and I wanted revenge."

My mind was blown. My mother had told me many times before how she held on to a lot of anger. But it never resonated with me because she was always so levelheaded and adored by everyone she'd ever met. Here she was telling me some of her darkest thoughts; she still hurt so badly nearly eighty years later.

"Do you still have those dreams?"

"No."

We both took a deep breath. And sat quietly for a moment.

"I wouldn't share these nightmares with my own mother because I didn't want her to be worried. But she could tell I wasn't right, so she'd say this little prayer in Hungarian to help me feel better. She'd say, 'Dear God, watch over us,' and she'd list all the people who had died, and it made me feel a little better. That list was long. The prayer would take a while to get through. But no matter how hard I tried, I couldn't shake that sick fantasy of wanting to burn down homes. It was twisted."

"Was it a Jewish prayer?"

"No! It rhymed. It was a rhyming prayer, at least in Hungarian."

My mom began to say something else and abruptly stopped.

"What were you going to say?"

"Never mind!"

"What? Tell me!"

"No, because I don't want it in the book."

"Why?"

"Because it's too sick."

I really wanted to know what she was about to tell me, but my stubborn mother would not budge. Over those years, people who know me well knew I'd often wish some not-so-kind things on people, most of whom worked in broadcast news. A lot of people in our business were promoted because of nepotism or, even worse, luck. There was no meritorious standard for success, and that always infuriated me, which propelled me to wish awful deaths on some. Did I regret this? Not really. Now, I wondered if I had inherited that gene from my mom. I imagine this is a toned-down version of what children of, let's say, serial killers deal with.

"Tell me! It needs to go in this book," I shouted at my mom, now getting worked up myself.

"No."

Our negotiations went into high gear. It was like a SWAT standoff with a barricaded wife killer. I was finally able to cajole my mom into a confession. As promised, I can't reveal it now, but she had another recurring, twisted fantasy about what she would do to the Nazis. It was dark, gruesome, and outright brutal, but it made me even more proud of my mom. I can't explain it. I was relieved, in an odd way, that she had this much anger at people who did the worst imaginable thing to her and her family and all the Jewish people. She would never forgive the Nazis, and I never ever wanted her to. Fuck them until eternity, and then some. You don't fuck with my family and my people. It was always my mom's attitude too, which is where I obviously got it from.

"And these fantasies came when you were just five?" I wanted to be sure.

"Yes."

"You admit you hold on to this anger today? Is it all still that raw?"

"Everybody was crying. Not for days, weeks, or months but for years. You know how many survivors don't like to talk about what happened? In my town, that's all they did. They talked about it incessantly."

"You just gave me a completely different answer from what I asked. Why are you still angry?

"Why am I still angry? Because death became part of my life when I was much too young. The Nazis tried to destroy us. They ruined families for generations upon generations."

We had just gone down a necessary rabbit hole. After hearing all this, I realized that it was even more poignant that my dad's death hit my mom harder than all the others. It underscored the strength of their bond, which had just become eternally unglued, at least from what it once was.

"When I saw your father that Monday morning, I knew it was the end game. Stop picking at your face!"

I had an itch in my left nostril and may have been trying to not-so-subtley pick it.

"Emaciated. He looked emaciated. He looked like he was at the absolute end. Stop picking your nose. How old are you?"

I got whatever it was that was causing the itch.

"I wasn't crying," my mom said as though she wanted to make it clear she was able to hold it together during the absolute worst of times.

Earlier that day, I had just seen my mom tear up and cry at the ANU museum. Why not when my dad was crossing over?

"You watched me choke up a few times today, right? In the museum. Yeah. Did you see me do that in the hospital or during the funeral? No, no you did not. So, help me understand why?"

"I think you've literally learned to turn off emotion like a spigot. You go into survival mode," I told her. We both knew why. But I think my mom needed reassurance in that moment that, despite her unemotive façade, she was still a warm, caring, and loving wife, mother, and human.

"When I got to Miami Jewish that day, I was ready for the end. I was ready for the end, and I knew I would have to handle the end."

My mom; my wife, Ileana; Lisandra; and I—of all the people my father had come across in his nearly ninety years, we were the only ones there in his final moments of life. The nurse told us she was having trouble getting a pulse. I was exhausted, reclining in a chair in the corner listening to the commotion as I battled to keep my eyes open and my hope alive.

"Stop picking your nose," my mom screamed. The itch was back. "I'm leaving if you don't stop it." I relented and sat on my hands to be able to get through the rest of this story.

"Suddenly, I told Eddie he could call in hospice. It was finally time. I was certain it would take another two or three days. Eddie told me he didn't have the hospice forms, and it was suddenly so chaotic. Doctors and nurses rushed in. Eddie was unfazed. He was working to get his pulse back. He was more relentless than I've ever been."

We both began to tear up in our dimly lit room eight thousand miles away in Tel Aviv.

"Thirty minutes later, he stopped breathing. None of us even knew. He just slipped away. It was so peaceful. He turned ashen. And I have no idea why, but I took a picture of him. It's not normal, I know. I wanted him to still be with me. I still frequently look at pictures of my own father who was gassed. I wanted to hold on to your father in the same way."

We were both full-on sobbing. I should've probably stood up and hugged my mom. But I was frozen by the emotion.

"Why did you take that pic?"

"No idea. No idea. And I'm not going to torture myself by trying to understand it. It's pretty crazy, I'll give you that. I haven't had the strength to go back and look at it. But it's in my phone still."

"In that very moment when he passed over to the other side, did you have a feeling, an emotion, a thought? Could you process it?"

"One of the worries I had was about you because you were sitting off to the side in a reclining chair. You weren't standing next to him to see exactly what was happening. And I knew you felt horrible about not being with Mabel when she died, and I didn't want you to freak out and get all emotional that he had just slipped away while you were exhausted on that chair."

It's amazing in a mother's worst moment that she can still worry about her child. I had just begun to feel that sort of self-less love with my own three young children. I never thought it was possible before.

After my dad's passing, we sat with his body. The rabbi who appeared explained that, according to Jewish law, he could not be left alone. My father looked a bit like a dart board with the number of needles still in his now lifeless body. But the rabbi told us that they could not be removed because not even a speck of blood can be unaccounted for as they would next prepare him for burial. The rabbi even instructed a nurse to wrap gauze around his head like a mummy to prevent any postmortem fluid from leaking out. I had never known any of this, now staring at my mummified dad with needles protruding from his body, which was quickly turning into a state of rigor mortis. I wondered how difficult it would be later to extract those needles from his hardened body. The things I think about.

THE FUNERAL...

By the following morning, after my dad took his final breath, my mom and I flew to New Jersey to reunite with my sister and her family for my dad's funeral. While I love my home state, spending eternity in Paramus, near one of the largest shopping malls, isn't too enviable. My poor father deserved better than to be a stone's throw from the Paramus Park Mall at the Cedar Park Cemetery. There were so many funerals there the day my father was buried that a family friend accidentally attended the wrong one unbeknownst to her until it was over. What a business death is.

"When you look back now, what did you think of the funeral?" I asked my mom roughly three months after the ignominious and final event.

"I was there, but I wasn't really there."

"Please don't give me these super short answers. This is a book, not a tweet," I again reminded my mom. She ignored me, rightfully.

"I felt like it's like a movie happening in front of me. I felt no pain, I felt no pain at all. In a very sick way, I was just glad you delivered a beautiful eulogy. So did your sister, Arden. I was really proud of you two."

"You kept repeating how happy you were that it was such a beautiful day. Why?"

"It was a beautiful sunny day, warm for that time of the year on March 29th. And I even slept well the night before. I think internally I felt that I accompanied him through life and took care of him. And now I was here with him for the bitter end. That gave me some comfort."

I've always been one to cling on to feelings of guilt. I wondered if my mom had any about my dad.

"I felt no guilt about something I didn't do or forgot to do. We pulled out everything we had to extend his life and keep him comfortable. I was there with him every single day because, as I said, I compulsively had to see him. I had to tell him I love him for those eight difficult months, and I had to hold his hand. I drove the nurses crazy. 'How is his hemoglobin?' 'Did he get fed?' 'Did you clear the mucous buildup from his throat?' 'Did you turn him from side to side?' He had to constantly be moved to prevent bed sores, which he got any way, and they were terrible at the end. His skin was like wet paper barely holding itself together. I annoyed the shit out of those nurses, and I feel good that I did."

Guilt had never been a driving force in my mother's life. It was a wasted emotion. And I knew she wasn't going to start feeling guilty with my father's death.

"He was dead man walking for eight months. But I'm so glad we had that extra time. I wish we had even more. I still just can't get over the finality of it all."

"There was a strange plot twist at Dad's funeral. The rabbi almost stepped on your son's headstone, which is embedded in the grass. Did you even know Rami was there right there just inches from Dad?"

All these years, my mom told me she didn't even know exactly where her son was buried. Now I wondered if she just said that to protect me because she didn't want me to visit and get saddened by it. As I mentioned earlier in the book, I had never ever visited Rami. This was an inauspicious moment to do it for the very first time.

"I knew he was buried there," my mom confessed, "but I hate cemeteries and never ever go. I will visit now, though."

It made me wonder selfishly if my mom would visit me if I beat her to the grave. I was about to ask her but was in no mood for the predictable backlash.

"Why do you hate cemeteries so much?"

"My father who was gassed in Auschwitz never had a grave. Maybe that's why. I felt cheated, maybe," my mom conjectured. "We just never had the tradition of going to grave sites. It was never a thing."

"Is there a memorial for him?"

I didn't know if I was a selfish bastard, disinterested, clueless, or all of the above, because I had never even wondered if my grandfather, murdered in Auschwitz, had a final resting place.

"He had no grave," my mom explained, "because he was incinerated in an oven after being so cruelly murdered. Your Grandma Anyu had his name engraved on his parents' headstone in Subotica. So, his name is written there, but that's it. Nothing more, nothing less."

"Does it make you angry that he doesn't have his own tombstone?"

"No, it makes me sad."

My mom began tearing up again. I had endearingly often called my mom "the ice queen" because of her unique ability to shut emotion off. She hated it.

"See I'm not an ice queen? I can cry too," my mom said proudly.

"Back to your son Rami. What was it like to see him right next to Dad?"

"I have one son. And he delivered a very nice eulogy. That baby of mine was a vegetable," she delineated starkly.

"How come you've always told me you didn't know where he was?" I obsessed over this.

"I swear I knew."

"So why didn't you ever tell me?"

"What's the point of visiting his grave? I don't believe the ones we loved are in the grave anyway. The only thing in the grave is a bunch of bones. That's it."

This was my mom: a harsh realist.

"By the way, what did you think of my eulogy? Was it trite? Was it profound?" I inappropriately fished for compliments at this most inopportune time.

"It was well written" is all she would give me.

"This isn't Twitter. Please expound." We both laughed.

"Because you are a writer. You write well. Your sister's speech was very nice too."

"Whose was better?" I asked without missing a beat.

"Oh, my aching ass, Joel. Your dad's funeral wasn't some sort of twisted sibling rivalry. You both did what you were supposed to, and you did it well."

"Were you pleasantly surprised that there was a good amount of people at the funeral?"

I spent a considerable amount of time worrying about who would show up to my father's funeral because all his friends, except maybe two, preceded him in death.

"I couldn't care less how many people were there. The rabbi was there, you and your sister were there, and that's all that matters. But it is nice that a lot of people paid their respects."

"One of the hardest things about a funeral for me is hearing the piles of dirt pounding the pine wood coffin. It's an eerie experience you cannot unhear."

"I didn't even notice it."

"You and I had to identify him. The rabbi lifted the coffin lid for us. That was the last time you'd ever see him. What was that like?"

"I never knew Jews put little pebbles on the eyes of the dead."

My mom never dwelled on anything, including seeing her husband for the very last time. She always kept moving forward, despite the difficulty of the circumstance. And this was as difficult as any circumstance would ever get for her.

"You had never heard of Jews putting little stones over the eyes of the dead?" I asked with a bit of surprise. At fifty-three, I still felt like my mom knew almost everything.

"Never. Never, never," she answered.

According to the educational website Classroom, it turns out, "the Jewish Mourning Guide notes that 'the eyes...should be closed, preferably by a firstborn son.' This tradition comes from Genesis 46:4, where Joseph closes his father Jacob's eyes upon the latter's death. Some modern Jews give the task of closing a parent's eyes to the child regardless of gender."

Who knew there was a "Jewish Mourning Guide"?

"Did he look at peace?"

"Yes, he looked completely at peace."

THE BIGGEST QUESTIONS...

"Where do you think Dad is now?"

"Nowhere. Absolutely nowhere. In the ground."

"I mean his soul," I clarified.

Jewish tradition believes in the "world to come." I've been saying Kaddish, the prayer for the dead, every day since his burial. Jewish teachings suggest that saying the prayer, which is invoked for eleven months, helps one's soul have an aliyah, or ascension to the heavens. I must admit I've struggled saying this prayer daily, wondering if it would actually help. Was I really helping raise his soul? It was something I was even afraid to question in case it really did happen, and now God might punish me for even bringing it up.

"I wish I could believe in the world to come. My mother believed it, may she rest in peace. My sister believes it. But I don't believe it," my mom confessed openly.

She wasn't worried at all about being struck down by a bolt of lightning for not buying into the belief hook, line, and sinker.

"Do you believe you'll see him again in another life? That you'll reunite and dance with your husband?"

"No. This is the very first time in my life I can mentally comprehend that death is final. It's irreversible and very, very, very final," my mom admitted.

"Do you feel guilty that you don't believe you'll see him again as Jewish tradition teaches?"

"I don't give a shit what some rabbi thinks of me. So, no I don't feel guilty. I feel sad. I feel that I lost something by not believing this." My mom, in her own distinct way, was admitting she wished she was more of a believer.

"Why don't you believe it?" I asked.

"It's a long story about why I don't believe it. The Jewish religion says that God takes care of each person on a very individualized level. The Buddhists believe different things. The Muslims believe yet other things, as do Christians. Personally,

I wish with all my heart that I could believe this, but I don't," she admitted.

I got teary-eyed that I may never ever see my own mother again once she was gone. Who can wrap their head around this?

"So where is Dad? What is Dad? Who, what is he now?"

"Nothing. He was. Now he's no more."

Of all the brutally harsh realities my mom shared with me on our fifty-three-year journey together as mother and son, this, without a doubt, was the most jarring.

"Do you worry that maybe if there is a God and he's hearing you, that he will exempt you from the afterlife for thinking this way?"

"You know, as I told you before, religious Jews say the afterlife only exists for those who believe in it."

"So maybe you want to fake it? I mean, you don't have *that* much longer to go," I joked with semi-serious intent.

"I can't fake it because if there is a God, then She knows that I'm faking it."

We laughed, which felt good right about now.

"Of all your losses, is this the hardest?"

My mom began crying.

"Without question. It's not even close. I was just cleaning out our place in New Jersey and found a note from him from years ago. It was beautiful. He wrote: 'My heart will always be yours. I love you.'"

I was now crying again too. I had always known my parents were madly in love with each other. But, until this very moment, I never fully understood how truly special this love really was.

I collected myself. And my mom snapped herself out of her long, unfettered gaze.

"You have no idea how loving and supportive of me he was and how much he cared about me and I cared about him," she reiterated, dabbing that stubborn tear from her eye. "I'll never say it was perfect, but it was pretty damn close."

"Do you find yourself angry in the same way you were with your own father's death? "

"No."

"Did you have enough time together?"

"Absolutely not. I want more, but it cannot be."

"So many people, when they find out someone has passed, feel compelled to tell you that person is now in a better place. Do you buy it?"

"No, but I appreciate the sentiment."

"What would you say to someone who just experienced a devastating loss?"

"I would tell them to think of all the wonderful things you experienced with that person. But your place is with the living now. It doesn't help to go into some sort of pathological mourning."

"Why must life include death too?" I asked because it always seemed so unfair to me, and still did, now more than ever.

"Because we are part of a cycle and death is a part of it. Renewing yourself after the death of someone you love is the key. It is so difficult, but it can be so wonderful. There can be some joy even in death, believe it or not."

If I had any worry my mother wouldn't survive the death of her own husband, it was all alleviated now. It was abundantly clear she would survive this too.

"Do you have hope for yourself after your husband's death?"

"Of course, I have hope for myself. I'm living through it all right now, aren't I?"

My mother is resilience personified. And it made me feel strong and proud.

"Where are you going?"

She started to get up, thinking we were done.

"I need to blow my nose. Is that allowed?"

"Yes, but wait one more minute," I pleaded. "During a quiet moment since Dad's death, have you broken down?"

"No. I'm sad and devastated. But I have not broken down."

"Why don't you think you've broken down?"

"Because this isn't the movies. I don't need to break down. I need to mourn in my own way, which is what I'm doing."

"Do you think the emotional avalanche will come?"

"I plan to get really depressed in the fall," my mom joked. "I'll tell you: the podcast is a lifesaver. It has given me real purpose and refocused me in a very positive, healthy way."

"Do you fear death after seeing what Dad went through?"

"I don't fear death."

"You're not just worried a little bit?"

"No. But I'll admit I do not like the concept of just disappearing and missing out on life. I really love this life, the good, the bad, and even the ugly."

"How do you remember Dad now?"

"I feel sad for him because he loved to live as much as me. But he lived his life with a high level of anxiety. For what? You see it all ends no matter what. So, enjoy the ride while you're on it and don't worry so much. I'm sad for him that he's gone."

The tears came streaming back down my face.

"He still exists if he lives in our minds," my mother comforted me, even though it was my time to console her.

"Your life started with so much death. And it appears to be ending with death now…"

"Who the fuck says I'm dying? Why do you keep burying me?" my mom interrupted as we both laughed, drying the tears from our eyes.

"Is it painful to know that you'll never hold his hand again or get a kiss from him?"

"Very, very, very, very, very, very, very, very, very painful. Very."

The tears were flowing. We were both a mess. But our conversation was so cathartic. We were vomiting up all of life's cruel bile and expelling it from our system.

"When I'm buried next to your dad, I want it written on both our tombstones: 'Our love will never die.'"

I jotted that down in my iPhone notes and included it in this book, so I'd never forget, and promised my mom I'd make it happen.

"Can you please stop asking me questions now?" my mom begged, exhausted both by the late hour and the draining subject.

"What's the moral of this story?"

"Like I said before, we can be sad for the dead, but our lives are with the living, and we must always pull strength from each other. We live in a beautiful world and, it's cliché, but it's true, we only get one chance at it."

"That's it?"

"Fuck off, Joel, you're draining me now."

"I'd hate to end the book this way. Are you sure you don't want to add one more thing? Do you think life is surreal?"

"No, it's just life. Enjoy it because soon enough we will all be dead."

Actual Voicemail from My Mom: June 19, 2023

We are on, I mean, at the airport.

What? Hello? What?

Sorry, I thought someone else was speaking.

I wanted to say goodbye to you. We all got into the El Al VIP lounge, even Beni, Arden, Raquel, and what's her name—my granddaughter Eden.

Remember to get health insurance for you and Ileana and the kids for when you meet me in Subotica.

And we love you, and we'll talk to you. Bye.

EPILOGUE—
"HITLER LOST"

It was an exceedingly hot, humid day in the former Yugoslavia and, despite where we were headed on that unforgetta- ble August day, I was ecstatic to see a bright red Yugo in the distance.

Despite the collective sadness we were about to feel as a family, this ugly, compact car brought a smile to my face. I hadn't seen one since they were first manufactured in the early 1980s and exported to the United States. I had a strange sense of pride about them because I knew they were from the same place as my mom—a place that had seemed as foreign then as it did now.

The Yugo was marketed as the first no-frills car. It came with no air conditioning, no power steering or roll-up windows. Now, I was staring at one in its natural habitat on a grassy knoll, not to be confused with the other more famous one, about twenty min- utes outside of Subotica, my mom's hometown, a place I never thought my family and I would ever actually visit.

But here we were.

Behind the Yugo was an old brick home, which look like it hadn't been touched since World War Two. As we arrived, a giant slovenly man, who ironically could never actually fit into a Yugo, emerged from the front door and greeted us warmly.

I could tell my children were scared of his unkempt, portly appearance while I was just mystified and curious about who he was. He spoke in a fast and furious pace with my aunt Betty, who was there to accompany us. His belly was so big that his pants could not be buttoned up, and his stained white textured tank top clung tight to his paunch, about seven inches short of his waistline, exposing his excessively hairy belly.

"Who is this guy?" I whispered to my mom, even though he didn't speak a lick of English.

"He's the cemetery caretaker," my mom informed me.

Still speaking quickly, he began pointing and wagging his hotdog-sized finger at an area behind his home so we all somewhat nervously headed in that direction. I had a flashback to my mom's story about my grandfather being led to the gas chamber and hoped this would have a more auspicious ending.

As we walked through knee-high grass, following the twists and turns of a few washed-out signs in a Cyrillic language, we came upon a black wrought-iron gate.

"This is it," my mom told us all.

"This is scary," my oldest daughter, Vida, remarked.

"We're fine," I told my kids, even though I wasn't sure I believed my own words.

Nearly eighty years after World War Two, I was standing at the entrance to my grandfather's final resting place. Well, sort of. His remains were never recovered because he was cremated after being sent to the Auschwitz gas chamber. Only his name—Laszlo Krishaber—was etched for all eternity in granite on the same headstone as my great-grandfather's. I couldn't comprehend that my grandfather—who had had such a profound impact on my life despite the fact that I never knew him—was right here in spirit.

"Where's the actual tombstone?" I curiously asked.

My mom was now speaking with the Serbian giant. It sounded like arguing to me, but as I had learned, this was just how they spoke to each other.

"He's not sure," my mom relayed to me.

"What?"

My wife was already through the wrought-iron gate looking for names on headstones. The cemetery extended in every direction. How were there so many dead Jews here, I wondered.

"Krishaber...with a K. Look for the letter K," my wife instructed our young children as they weaved through rows and rows of the dead.

"Here's a Krishaber," my wife shouted with elation.

My mom, noticeably a bit nervous and in a somewhat typical state of agitation, zig-zagged her way through the high grass to take a closer look.

"Wrong Krishaber," she announced flatly.

The search continued.

"Here's another Krishaber!" my wife yelled.

I was pissed I hadn't found one yet, while simultaneously confused about how there could be this many Krishabers in this one cemetery. A name I had not heard before or since finding out about my grandfather.

"Not ours," my wife said upon taking a closer look.

Had we really all traveled more than five thousand miles to be unable to find my grandfather's name in this random plot of land in this undeniably remote part of Serbia?

"We tried. It's hot," my mom said.

"Are you serious? We just traveled halfway around the globe to see my grandfather and their great-grandfather," I argued incredulously as I pointed to my children.

"Is this it?" my wife screamed yet again from another row of worn, tattered and chipped headstones.

Somewhat reluctantly, my mom headed over to check out this latest discovery. She stared at the large, black granite stone. She peered in closer to read the Serbian inscription. It looked like it had been polished recently—one of the few with this distinction. The sunlight was reflecting off of it, creating a beam of light heavenward.

"I can't believe my aching ass," my mom said, "this is it!"

"This is my grandfather?" I asked, staring at this giant slab of stone from a different era.

"It's just his name. He's not here. These are your great-grandparents," my mom reminded me. "Only his name is inscribed here."

She stared at the headstone intently. She seemed to be in deep thought.

"What the hell do I know? Maybe his spirit is here! Those goddamn Nazis may they rot in hell."

We stood respectfully. We were all silent. I wanted to cry but couldn't. Neither could my mom.

Prior to our arrival, I had told my children that Jewish tradition was to lay stones on gravesites in the belief it would keep the soul down in this world.

Moments later Vida, Zizi, and Judah appeared cradling piles of stones in their small arms and asked if they could place some on their great-grandfather's headstone.

"Yes."

My three children were now honoring the man who created my mom, ergo me and them, but who subsequently lost his life for one reason: being Jewish.

"Hitler lost," I said to my mom. "Vida, Zizi, and Judah are living proof he couldn't destroy us as a people."

Back in Miami Beach, we reminisced about the trip of a lifetime I don't think any of us thought we'd actually ever go on. It had only been a few months, but it already seemed as long ago to me as World War Two.

"Subotica reminded me of a gingerbread town. How come you always downplayed it as this place filled with Serbian peasants?" I asked.

"You saw it in summer, not the dead of winter."

"The town square is beautiful," I countered.

"It is. I'll give you that. The town square is stunning."

My wife documented our entire journey on Instagram. It served at least one positive function, I thought. Our friends all messaged us telling us they wanted to visit too—they couldn't believe how incredibly beautiful and quaint Subotica was. It wasn't at all what I expected.

"What did you think of the old man we met in front of your childhood home?"

All these places, which had once just been nebulous pieces of my family history, were now real in my mind. I had seen the most important places in my mother's childhood firsthand with my very own eyes. I had stood before the house that my great-grandfather built for my grandfather and grandmother when they got married.

"It was weird to meet that man," my mom admitted.

Her childhood home was on a quiet, tree-lined street. This was where the Nazis had grabbed my grandfather at his front door. I touched that door. At once, it was somehow both real yet so surreal and difficult to process.

"It's a miracle that it wasn't torn down. All the other old houses were torn down and apartments were built in their place. But our house is still there all these years later," my mom couldn't believe it herself.

"What did that old man say to you?"

Seemingly out of nowhere appeared a man in his nineties dressed in a fine European suit with a fedora from a period of time that had long predated our chance meeting.

"He simply told me that the reason he's lived so long is because he is an optimist."

Maybe it was worth it to switch over to the other side, I thought, questioning my own unrelenting cynicism. At least I might live a few more years if I suddenly became an optimist.

"Did you think that he was some sort of symbol of divine intervention put in our path that day to remind us that there was still good in the world despite all the evil and hardship you experienced firsthand?"

"No." My mom was never the type to buy into dramatic hyperbole. "It was an interesting little encounter—that's it. But he was straight out of central casting, wasn't he?"

We had also visited the house my mom returned to after being hidden during the war.

It was a large home with three big apartments attached to it. We met distant relatives of my mom who were still living there all these years later.

We're all now connected on Facebook, and these people too are no longer just characters in stories about my mom's past.

We also visited the gingerbread-looking synagogue I had heard so much about in previous conversations about my mom's past. It was stunning.

"Who was the woman who grabbed your face with both hands?" I had already forgotten her story.

"It was a woman whose mother knew my grandfather. Even when there were eight thousand Jews living in Subotica, it was small. Everyone knew everyone. She was just excited to see me all these years later."

The best of writers, of which I'm far from, would find trouble describing my mom's childhood synagogue. It reminded me a bit of pictures I've seen of Moscow's Kremlin. It was big and beautiful with unusual architecture—something you'd never see anywhere in America. The inside was even more impressive. It was cavernous, with Sistine Chapel–style painted ceilings that seemed to extend to the heavens. There were impeccably maintained, carved wooden rows of benches, which used to be filled with Jews praying, left empty after the war, now just a Serbian historical landmark.

"What was it like to be in there with your grandchildren?"

"It was emotional. You have to give the Serbs credit for the way they restored and maintained the synagogue."

"Was it badly destroyed during the war?" I asked, realizing I had never even considered this as a possibility before visiting it myself.

"It wasn't destroyed. It was just worn by life, by time—sort of like me," my mom half-joked.

"What happened to the Jewish community?"

"You saw it."

The day we were there, a small group of people were playing cards in a backroom. There were maybe a dozen remaining congregants.

"It's basically just a small community center now," my mom explained, her sadness evident in her tone.

Eight thousand Jews now reduced to just this handful of card players, finding some enjoyment, in a place where their past had been so excruciatingly and painfully erased.

If it weren't for righteous Gentiles, my mom wouldn't be here today.

Non-Jews saved my mom and thereby allowed for my existence in this crazy world, and now, the existence of a new generation—my own children. I wish I could've personally thanked all of those non-Jews in Subotica, but the passing of time had made this wish impossible to fulfill.

"The Catholic school you were hidden in was sort of creepy. The kids were terrified."

My mom didn't know exact addresses or street names anymore. So, we found many of the places so important to her past through intuition. As we walked, she followed memories and hunches to get to what we were looking for.

"It's on a creepy street," my mom admitted about the Catholic school that Dr. Sercer had led her to when she was just four and a half years old back in 1943.

"That's where you famously yelled at your mother for abandoning you?"

"I screamed that a mother who loves her children doesn't leave them with strangers."

Now I knew the place she was speaking of. I had now been there, too, and even smelled the summer air on that creepy street, walking the same path my mom had taken so many years earlier—one that changed her life forever. But, as hard as I tried, I still couldn't fathom that all this history had unfolded, right there, in that spot, changing my family forever.

"What was it like to be back there?"

"I feel good that I could show it to you and my grandchildren. Especially because I had always described it as having a big door, and I was right. It had a big door."

My mom always loved to be right.

"Never again" was the famous refrain after so many Jewish lives were lost during the Holocaust.

But incredibly, as we were recapping our summer trip to Subotica, my mom was now trying to wrap her head around what she described as another pogrom.

Fourteen hundred Jews were slaughtered October 7th and hundreds taken hostage in Israel's own version of 9/11.

The country my mother loved more than anything, arguably as much as her own family, now found itself at war. My nephews Joe and Yaron, reservists in the IDF, left their own families to protect Israel's northern border.

"What is your response to what happened in Israel on October 7th?"

"I don't have a normal reaction."

"What's your *abnormal* reaction?"

Earlier in this book, for better or worse, my mom admitted it was harder for her to leave Israel than lose her terminally ill son Rami.

"I'm very angry Israel let it happen. This was such a fuck-up by intelligence. I was there when the Yom Kippur War broke out, and that was fifty years ago to the day from this event."

"I was there too. I'm fifty-four."

"Oh yeah, I forgot about you," she said, laughing along with me.

"Back then, it was very hard to understand how Israel got caught with their pants down. And now history is repeating itself. I'm too old for this shit."

"You get upset with me whenever I engage in what you describe as self-destructive behavior. Do you feel like the Israelis were self-destructive by not anticipating this attack?"

"It was pure neglect."

"Were you more upset at the Israelis or those cancerous cretins Hamas, if you're being honest?"

"I'm more upset the Israelis let this happen. This was a stupid, stupid, stupid oversight. It was neglect."

My mom had choice words too for the terrorists responsible—Hamas.

"Hamas is worse than the Nazis. Everyone's arguing if they beheaded babies. It's not bad enough they burned them? They need to be beheaded? I'm sure they did that too. They're animals who need to be destroyed. And Israel will make them pay the ultimate price."

"What about the Palestinians in Gaza?"

I wasn't sure what to expect with this answer.

"I feel badly for the Palestinian children."

"You do?"

"Yes."

One-word answers from my mom always only meant one thing: she was angry.

"All children should be protected no matter what."

Anti-Israel protests erupted globally. Antisemitism has risen to all-time highs. It seemed like the entire world was out to get the Jews again.

"Did you know this many people hate the Jews?"

My mom stared me dead in the eyes and didn't answer. She knew that I knew all these people wanted us dead and gone.

"Do these protests bother you?"

"I'm immune." She gave me two words now. I was getting somewhere.

"We're the most hated people on earth, Joel. But I have news for the entire world. We're not going anywhere. The Jews are too smart. The Israeli military is too advanced, too powerful, and the IDF will be unrelenting in its response to this. The world is about to find this out firsthand."

In the worst of times, my mom always found her greatest strength, and this time was no exception.

"Israel is such a small country that there's, quite literally, not enough room to write 'Israel' on the map. The Arab countries surrounding us are so much bigger in size, but we are so much greater in every other way. As the saying goes, 'It's kill or be killed,' and the latter is not an option for us."

"Do you wish you could fight for Israel?" I asked playfully.

"I'd kill whoever I need to for Israel's survival," she answered like she was ready, in that very moment, to switch places with my nephews on the frontlines.

"Do your grandchildren give you hope?"

My mom who has eight grandchildren also just recently became a great grandmother to Roey, named after my father Roy. His father Joe is the one fighting for Israel.

The circle of life has never been more apparent to me than as I type these final words.

"The fact I survived the Holocaust is luck. I wasn't even five years old when I was forced to escape. And I wasn't even six when I came back to my home. I think I drew a lucky number in the life lottery. You know, I could just as easily have been gassed like the other one and a half million Jewish children. I repeat: one and a half million Jewish children. Do you know how many children that is?"

My mom had always begged me to give more and take less. And now I was finally doing just that. I was feeling so happy, an emotion I typically found so elusive, that one day I could give this very book to my own children to read so they could learn all about their grandmother who was a miracle to us and so many other lives she touched. She remains a force of nature.

"Even though my kids are only nine, seven and four, what would you say to them when they're twenty-six, twenty-four, and twenty-one?"

"Nothing makes me happier than seeing the three of you. What wonderful people you have become and how caring and loving and smart and beautiful you are. I have so much peace leaving you in this world because I know you are going to do the right things."

At the beginning of this book, I described my mom as a gift for the entire world to unwrap, but especially her own grandchildren.

And now this remarkable woman was speaking directly to them—and hopefully their children, and their children's children—and everyone's children as this ever-revolving circle of life continues to spin relentlessly, but beautifully, into the future.

"I know you are all going to have a big heart and do beautiful things that you're so capable of. I love you all very, very much. And when you think of me, you should know that I had a very good life despite a few tragedies like the Holocaust and losing a child. I had a very loving husband. I had two wonderful children. I enjoyed my work as a therapist and all my friendships I developed along the way, and I enjoyed taking care of all of you. My life was so, so good. I loved the movies. I loved reading even more. I loved traveling and seeing the world and meeting so many interesting people. Enjoy every second, even the bad, because it all goes too damn fast! Now it's your turn to live!"

POSTSCRIPT

Dear Reader:

After I read this manuscript I felt embarrassed by my use of four-letter expletives.

I decided to work on eliminating curse words.

Hopefully, I still have time to change.

Fondly,
Karmela

Karm's Synagogue in Subotica, Serbia

My grandfather Laszlo Krishaber's cemetery

תנצבה

KRISZHÁBER ÁRMIN
1872–1941.
KRISZHÁBER LÁSZLÓ
1910–1944
AUSCHWITZ

Subotica Town Square

The house Karm grew up in before World War II

The Catholic school Karm was hidden in

Laszlo Krishaber's optometry diploma. It was because of this that he was sent to the Auschwitz gas chambers.

ACKNOWLEDGMENTS

Surviving the Survivor is a book and eponymous true crime podcast that is so much bigger than just my dear mother and me. It's truly a team effort.

My sister, Arden Fusman, has always been massively supportive of everything I've ever done. My mother loves us equally despite pressing her to admit otherwise in the preceding pages. Her husband, Beni, and my nieces Lior, Hana, Judi, Raquel, and Eden are always rooting for our success, too. My uncles Seymour and Ron, aunts Naomi and Elizabeth, and cousins Michah, Eyal, Tamar, and Sylvia and Nina.

My in-laws are amazingly encouraging, too. Thank you to Sandy, Mario, Karla, Matt, Mario Jr., Alex, Ito, Gisy, Johnny, Rita, Erik, Manny, Gabby, Tia Mirella, Mirella Maria, Randy, Angel & Eduardo.

Everything good in life begins with a strong foundation. Highland Park, New Jersey inspired me in ways that are difficult to articulate. There's no better place in the world to grow up.

I'd like to thank my hometown friends whose own, unbelievable success always drove me to do better: Michael Littman, Howard Schweitzer, Steve Isakoff, Rob Crozier, John Hulme and Steve Chudnick. David Kamp is a literary talent like no other who knew exactly how to craft the wording for this very book cover. We were all taught by Bob Stevens, may he continue to rest in peace. Teachers make a huge difference in everyone's lives; a career that deserves more respect and way more money. While I'm at it, shoutout to Highland Pizza, Tastee Subs and White Rose—Central Jersey Institutions. And, of course, Carmen Crea at Haven. And thanks to other Highland Parkers who helped me along the way: Marci Lerner, Sharon Kroll Cohen, Eva Hoffman Cornick, Jodi Mitnick Toubes, Matt Kaufman. And Rob Feldman, the smartest person I've ever known, and Josh Mitnick, a tenacious and dogged journalist, who left us way too soon.

It's hard to get people to take chances on you. Publisher of Post Hill Press Anthony Ziccardi took a blind leap of faith having only really known my work as an investigative reporter for Fox 5 NYC. It's difficult to express how grateful I am to him for taking this gamble on me. Post Hill's Maddie Sturgeon helped me every step of the way and was always extremely knowledgeable and gracious. I'm now an author, a lifelong dream, because of you two and everyone who makes the magic happen at Post Hill Press.

Surviving the Survivor, the podcast with the #BestGuests in #TrueCrime, is truly a team effort. Both the book and show would be impossible without the COE (Chief of Everything), also known as my wife, Ileana. Legendary network news booking producer Steve "Meve Moen" Cohen is a big part of the reason we deliver the most compelling content on any platform anywhere. Spaced Coast on the West Coast is an audiophile and tech wizard who ensures the quality of our programming is always next to none. And, of course, our amazing mods: IAmNotTPain, Frankie Figs, GenXGranny, NJ's CopperHorse, and Shaquille Oatmeal. Thank you for always working so diligently. And of course, STS Nation, our beloved community.

From the United States to England, Canada to Gambia, Nepal to the North Pole and New Zealand, Australia to South Africa, the Netherlands, India, Mexico, Central and South America, and of course the Republic of Ireland and Tasmania, you are the best of the best. We'd be nothing, literally, without all of you.

I'd also like to thank my skin for growing somewhat thicker over the years. As a former broadcast news correspondent and current podcaster, the vast majority of public sentiment is overwhelmingly positive. However, I tend to hear the criticism more. So, thanks to all the haters. You always motivated me to prove you wrong. I'm sure I'm still not there yet. But it's a work in progress. It's why I opened this book with a quote from my mother: "The dogs bark and the caravan passes."

To my children, Vida, Zizi, and Judah, I cannot imagine life without you. Listen to grandma: let those dogs bark loudly but always keep your caravan moving forward steadily and assuredly. I love you more than is articulable.

Lastly, my mother has also always told me we're all just trying to survive in a rough world. It is true. We have no idea what is really going on with those surrounding us. So, make it a point to be kind and empathetic to all. Most people struggle silently. So always be loud with your compassion.

Love ya America and everyone and everywhere near and far between.

ABOUT THE AUTHOR

J oel Waldman is the co-host of the hit true-crime podcast *Surviving the Survivor* and an Emmy Award-winning broadcast journalist who worked most recently as a Washington, D.C.-based correspondent for Fox News, covering national politics from Capitol Hill. He has also worked as an investigative reporter for Fox 5 in New York City and for TV-news programs in West Palm Beach, Miami, and Tucson. He lives in Miami Beach with his wife, Ileana, and his three children, Vida, Zizi, and Judah.